God Comes to
Women

God Comes to Women

HEATHER FARRELL & JEN MABRAY

CFI
An imprint of Cedar Fort, Inc.
Springville, Utah

A special thanks goes to Paige Winfree
for her beautiful illustrations.

"The cover art is a powerful reflection of the stories inside this book. Much like the doves coming down from above, Heavenly Father guided my mind with a clear image of how to present my own witness that God comes to women."

—Paige Winfree

ISBN 13: 978-1-4621-3998-9

Published by CFI, an imprint of Cedar Fort, Inc.
2373 W. 700 S., Springville, UT 84663
Distributed by Cedar Fort, Inc., www.cedarfort.com

Library of Congress Control Number: 2021932778

Cover design by Courtney Proby
Cover design © 2021 by Cedar Fort, Inc.

Printed in the United States of America

10 9 8 7 6 5 4 3 2 1

Printed on acid-free paper

Contents

A NOTE FROM THE AUTHORS

Before you begin reading about how God comes to women, we want to share a beautiful aspect of the theology of The Church of Jesus Christ of Latter-day Saints; that God is not just male but a divine couple, a Heavenly Father and a Heavenly Mother, perfectly unified as one. In the first chapter of Genesis we learn, "God created man in his *own* image, in the image of God created he him; male and female created he them" (verse 27). If both men and women are created in the image of God, then it stands to reason that the "image" (a word which in Hebrew means "form") of God encompasses both female and male aspects.

We do not worship multiple Gods; we worship *one* God, who is both perfectly male and perfectly female.[1] While we believe that Heavenly Father and our Heavenly Mother are separate, each having their own male and female body, yet they are, in some cosmic way, still *one*.[2] Though we do not quite understand how it is possible, our Heavenly Father and Heavenly Mother are more unified than we can really comprehend.

In recent years there has been a surge in Christian art featuring a Heavenly Mother, and while much of it is beautiful and inspirational, She is often depicted by Herself.[3] If we were to paint a different picture of our Heavenly Mother, it would not be of Her as a lone, independent goddess, but rather as a divine partner, perfectly unified with our Heavenly Father. In fact, our prophet and apostles often use the phrase "Heavenly Parents" to refer to God. The Young Women theme was also adapted to reflect this emphasis on Heavenly Parents, the perfect unity between male and female.

It is also important to remember that the only way that we have access to God—God the Father or God the Mother—is through Their Son, Jesus Christ. First Timothy 2:5 states, "There is one God, and one mediator between God and men, the man Christ Jesus." Jesus Christ is our advocate with the Father and with the Mother, and if we want to know either of Them, the way is through Their Son, Jesus Christ. If we want to know Her nature and power, we must study the life and nature of Her Son. In Him is a portion of the image of Her, in the same way children resemble the image of each of their parents. As we come to know Him better, we come to better understand the Father *and* the Mother. The Son is the way.

As you read this book, we want you to keep in mind that the God we speak of encompasses both the masculine and the feminine, our Divine Father and our Divine Mother—perfectly unified as *one*.

Introduction

[Women] should seek the Lord, if haply they might feel after him, and find him, though he be not far from every one of us: for in him we live, and move, and have our being.

—ACTS 17:27–28

A Message from Heather Farrell

The idea for this book blossomed out of a conversation Jen and I had one afternoon over Zoom. It was the middle of lockdown due to the Covid-19 pandemic, and Jen had reached out to me about an article she was writing on Book of Mormon women. During our conversation I expressed to Jen the discouragement I was feeling. We had endured almost a month of complete isolation due to the Covid-19 virus, and I, with my houseful of small children, was feeling overwhelmed by it. The temples were closed, we had not been able to attend church, and I had not been able to be truly alone for over a whole month. No matter where I went in my home, there was always someone who needed me.

At one point I'd even tried to hike up in the woods on the mountain behind our house to find some peace and quiet in which to pray. I imagined that like Joseph Smith I would find my own sacred grove where I could speak openly to my Father in Heaven. Yet the momentary peace I found was quickly shattered by two little girls who, as soon as they realized I was gone, stood on the back porch and screamed my name until I came back. Joseph Smith had to contend with forces of darkness, but I had to contend with the combined forces of a two-year-old and a four-year-old.

As I hiked back down the mountain, I thought about how in the scriptures it is usually men who go to the mountains or wilderness to commune with God—Moses, Nephi, Abraham, Enos, John the Baptist,

1

Joseph Smith. Why weren't there any stories of women who had gone to the mountain, women who had communed with God? I was pretty sure I knew why. Their lives were probably even more burdened with people and responsibilities than mine. Maybe it was just as hard, or even harder, for them to find time to be with God as it was for me. It seemed supremely unfair that perhaps women—all throughout history—had missed out on mountaintop interactions with God, simply because they could not leave behind their family responsibilities.

I complained about all of this to Jen, expecting that she would join me in lamenting the challenges of being a woman, especially one with children. Instead her words took me by surprise: "Heather, that is why God comes to women. Men must climb the mountain to be with God, but God comes to women where they are." When she said those words, a little thrill went up my spine, and I felt all my bitterness melt away as the truth of what she said sank into my heart.

God does indeed come to women. I knew this because He had come to me, not always in majestic manifestations on the mountaintop, but in small, quiet ways. I remembered how, just a few days earlier, I had felt the impression to turn off the radio while I was driving in the car and to just listen. In those few quiet moments I'd felt God beside me, sitting in the seat next to me as I drove, speaking peace to my heart and renewing my soul. It was a simple experience, but when I took time to reflect on it I saw that even in the bustle of my life, He had found a way to come to me.

In the scriptures we also find that God often interacted with women, not on the mountain, but at the wells where they drew water for their families, in their homes, in their kitchens, in their gardens. He came to them as they sat beside sickbeds, as they gave birth, as they cared for the elderly, and as they performed necessary mourning and burial rites. When women's hearts were seeking Him, He came to them; no matter where they were or what they were doing.

This idea of God coming to women sank deep into my heart. Several days later, on Easter Sunday, I wrote about our conversation in a post that I shared on Instagram.[4] I was astounded when just a few hours later I began to get texts and emails from family, friends, and even distant acquaintances saying they had seen the post and were very moved by it. I checked Instagram and Facebook and saw that in just a few hours the post had been shared thousands of times! In the following weeks and months it would go on to be re-shared over social media, email, and by text to *millions* of people. The message was even translated into several different languages and was widely circulated—not just among Latter-day Saints circles, but by Christians all over the world.

Interestingly, as the post circulated, the original picture I included was changed, and instead the words were often accompanied by a photo of a woman standing at the sink doing dishes. I saw the post shared several different times, each with a different picture of a woman doing dishes. This common interpretation made me smile because it captured so beautifully what Jen and I had talked about; that, in the hustle and bustle of our lives, we often experience God in the quiet moments in between. The moments when our hearts reach out to Him as we are doing the most ordinary things.

So much of the work women do, and have done for millennia, is service to other people. And as King Benjamin taught, "When you are in the service of your fellow beings, you are only in the service of your God" (Mosiah 2:17). Jesus also said something similar: "Inasmuch as ye have done it unto the least of these my brethren, ye have done it unto me" (Matthew 25:40). The service that women give is service to God, and He sees it, recognizes it, and visits women when they are about His work.

It is important to note that even though this book is called *God Comes to Women* and we are focusing on the ways in which God speaks and appears to women, it does not minimize the fact that God comes to men as well. We have examples in the scriptures of both men *and* women who were visited by God while they were doing ordinary things. For example, the disciples Peter, James, and John were fishermen who, right in the middle of their daily work, were invited by Christ to follow Him and become "fishers of men" (Matthew 4:19). God is no respecter of persons and speaks openly to all those who seek him, both male and female.

Our prophet, Russell M. Nelson, has been encouraging us to learn to "hear Him," to recognize God's voice in our life and obey His will. President Nelson said, "Our efforts to *hear Him* need to be ever more intentional. It takes conscious and consistent effort to fill our daily lives with His words, His teachings, His truths."[5] Jen and I hope that in this book you will learn to see and recognize the ways in which God speaks to you, visits you, and gives you personal revelation, whether it be on the mountaintop or down in the valley.

God speaks to each of us differently. As you study the stories of women, ancient and modern, who have heard, seen, and interacted with God, our hope is that your ability to hear, see, and interact with Him will increase. We have even included some journaling pages in the back of this book for you to reflect and record ideas and experiences that come to you as you read.

Remember, God comes to women. He knows where we are and understands the burdens we carry. He sees us, and if we open our eyes and reach our hearts toward His, we will find Him, even in the most ordinary places and in the most ordinary things.

A Message from Jen Mabray

As I contemplated how I came to this belief that God comes to women, I realized my journey started long ago. When I was twenty-one years old, I became interested in developing a relationship with God, and I was willing to transform my actions and behavior to see what was possible with Him. Actually, it was more than that. I was at a crossroads, and I decided I *had* to have a relationship with Him.

My relationship with my own father was almost always in turmoil, and I wanted to discover whether a relationship with my Heavenly Father could be different, honorable, wholesome, and endearing. The best idea I could come up with to start my journey with God was to begin with a simple prayer. I petitioned God to help me learn about Him, and most important to me at the time, who I was to Him. That intentional desire started me on a journey that has filled my life with many personal experiences with God, ranging from simple conversations in prayer to the recognition of His profound strength and healing power in my life. In the last twenty years since my simple prayer, I have learned to treasure His attention that encompasses companionship, instruction, laughter, reproof, and love.

One of my most treasured and joyful experiences with God happens to be with, of all things, an armadillo. I have shared my armadillo story many times with the youth of the Church in the last decade. It's one of my favorite experiences to show how endearing and attentive our Father in Heaven is to each of us.

Years ago, my husband Todd and I purchased compound bows and decided we would compete for our first animal. Months later, we were on a friend's property playing outdoor games with our kids, and I sailed my arrows across a large field. As I walked back from retrieving my arrows, I heard something rustle in the underbrush of the tree line next to me. Little creatures, boars, and even bobcats were common in those woods, so

I knocked an arrow for safety and quietly continued to follow the sound. My mind filled with an image of me walking back with a deer slung over my shoulder like those slow-motion scenes from the action movies.

I stepped a little, and it stepped a little. Finally, after several minutes of following the sound, I saw it! To my dismay, it was only an armadillo but my adrenaline was already pumping and my fingers were ready to draw that knocked arrow.

Todd was sitting nearby with the kids and I whispered, "Todd . . . there's an armadillo."

He responded, "So?"

"Can I shoot it?" I asked, still whispering.

"I don't care." He shrugged.

Apparently, he had forgotten about our little bet, or maybe the bet was only for some prized animal, like a deer or a wild turkey. Regardless, there before me was my first animal . . . *an armadillo*. I drew my bow, lined up my sights, held my breath, and released the string. My arrow pierced the little guy through, and he quickly fell dead. The adrenaline in my body was like nothing else! Not only did I win the bet, but I also nailed the little guy from several yards away!

Don't laugh too much, but later that evening, my adrenaline quickly melted into guilt and tears. *I just killed an innocent armadillo! What the heck was I thinking?* I couldn't shake the guilt and when I complained to Todd, his response was, "Jen, it's just an armadillo, it's fine." But his words did not pacify me, so I decided to talk to the Lord.

In my library, I began to petition the Lord for forgiveness in prayer. "Heavenly Father . . . I shot an armadillo today, on purpose, and . . . " Immediately I burst into out-loud laughter. Instinctively, I looked up at the ceiling because I felt like Heavenly Father was laughing too! A little confused as to what just happened, I left my library and explained to my husband that I had just tried to pray about the armadillo, and I felt like Heavenly Father was laughing about it. Todd also burst into laughter and said, "Well, Jen, it is kinda funny how much you're crying over this armadillo."

"No, it's not!" I stammered. "I feel really bad, and both of you guys are just laughing! I'm going to try again." But as soon as I began my second attempt to ask for forgiveness, the same laughter came down from heaven. In a strange combination of full laughter and sorrowful tears, I said aloud, "Heavenly Father, I'm trying to apologize and you think it's funny! It's not funny. I'm really sorry I killed the armadillo. I feel really bad." Moments later, a peace flooded my mind and heart, and I felt these words: "Jen, I love you, and it really *is* pretty funny how much you are worried about the armadillo. It is true, the animals are not for target practice, but you need not worry any longer."

I never tire of thinking about the armadillo story. It still makes me laugh, and it changed my perspective of God. I feel like He showed me a side of His personality I had never before considered. When God comes to us, He laughs with us and is willing to be in the details of our lives, even over something so insignificant and small. In just a moment with Him, He taught me how to better recognize Him and ultimately, that He is not an unapproachable or unrelatable entity.

The impact of the armadillo story on my life acted as a springboard into another journey to learn about God, this time through my education. When I began my graduate work in Jewish studies, Hebrew, and Jewish literature, I felt at odds with canonized and sacred texts that contain mostly masculine encounters with God in contrast to a low number of recorded feminine encounters with God. Likely due to social and cultural boundaries, often only divine encounters between God and men were preserved and typically from the male perspective. Except for a few highly praised Jewish matriarchs and early disciples of Christ, women traditionally occupied supportive roles in canonized texts and sometimes they were not approached or believed when they had encounters with the Divine. However, this did not mean women did not experience God. I began to wonder if there was another "half" of Godly encounters with His children. Where was the *women's* half? Beautifully, and thankfully, canonized and sacred texts are replete with divine visitations to men and some women, yet in my opinion, they still contain only a "half-portion" of the world's narratives detailing encounters with God.

From this perspective, I contemplated my own experiences with God and the hundreds of private one-on-one conversations I've had with women who have shared with me *their* experiences with Him. I have sat with women in living rooms, bedrooms, front porches, cars, seminary classrooms, restaurants, chapels, and chatted on the phone listening to their treasured and often sacred stories with God which proved to me that women also experience God perfectly, beautifully, and completely. I believe that any perceived or actual imbalance of women's voices in scriptural canons does not mean women have minimal encounters with

God. Women have experiences with God all the time, and many of our stories are as extraordinary as those recorded in sacred canons! He comes to women in prayers, dreams, feelings, and thoughts; through angelic helpers—both mortal and immortal—and during experiences with conception, pregnancy, motherhood, sisterhood, death, ministering, and companionship with others. He comes to women not less often, not less clearly, but differently. Our privilege is to explore how He comes to us.

Today, I feel the "women's-half" of the world's narratives detailing encounters with the Divine is yet to be fully written, preserved, and disseminated for others to contemplate and study. Currently, this "hidden-half" of significant and treasured experiences with God resides in the hearts and memories of women.

Heather and I wrote this book as a starting point in the preservation of women's experiences with God. We hope the stories and scriptural interpretations in our chapters will feed your soul and cause you to recall and rejoice in your own experiences with Him. The stories are real. And we testify that God really does come to women.

When You Can't Climb the Mountain

by Heather Farrell

*"Draw near unto me and I will draw
near unto you; seek me diligently
and ye shall find me."*

—DOCTRINE AND COVENANTS 88:63

When I was fourteen years old my Young Women group went on a grueling hike. Our destination was the top of a high plateau that had a spectacular view of the surrounding mountain range. The ascent was steep and difficult, and after several hours of climbing one of our leaders had to turn back. Her body simply could not take her any farther. Sobbing, she was escorted slowly back down the mountain by one of the priesthood leaders who had accompanied us.

Several hours later, and after completing one of the hardest physical challenges of my young life, I found myself standing on top of a mountain. The view from the top was spectacular; it literally took my breath away. Standing up there, my perception of things was so different. Things that had seemed big and important now seemed tiny and insignificant in the face of so much grandeur and majesty. The air was different, thinner and colder, and full of reverence. As my head brushed the tops of clouds, I understood why in the scriptures the temple was referred to as the "mountain of the Lord." The mountain was as near as you could get to piercing the veil, parting the clouds, and seeing God.

When we came down off the mountain we were greeted by our leader who had waited for us to return. As we eagerly told her about our hike and about the incredible view from the top, she smiled, hugged us, and told us she was proud of us. Only years later, as a grown woman, have I realized how hard that must have been for her. She had wanted to reach the top too. She had wanted to stand in the clouds and feel the majesty of God surrounding her but had been unable to, not because her will was not strong enough but because her physical body was simply not capable of carrying her there. The mountaintop had been completely out of her reach.

Sometimes as women we may feel like we are missing out on potential spiritual experiences because we are unable to climb the mountain. We find it hard to physically separate ourselves from the people, things, and circumstances of our lives. We have babies who need us every hour of the day, children who demand our attention, spouses who need an equal partner, aging parents who cannot be left alone, neighbors who are in need, and the responsibility of dozens of daily tasks necessary to sustain physical life. One of my favorite authors, Pearl S. Buck, wrote about the struggle her mother had between the desire to live a more "spiritual" life and the pressing reality of caring for physical needs. Buck's mother, named Carrie, and her husband, Andrew, were Christian missionaries in China during the last part of the nineteenth century. Buck wrote:

> Andrew, laboring over their everlasting souls, would not have thought of lice and bedbugs. Carie, engrossed in the necessity for cleanliness, saw Andrew praying with some refractory lad and paused to think remorsefully, "How much better he is than I! How is it I forget so about souls". But the next moment her interest would be caught in the ordering of rice and vegetables or there would be a little boy who looked pale and she must coax him to drink a little milk . . . , or there would be itch on another's hands and she must run for the sulphur mixture. Souls were more important, that one [she] believed heartily, but bodies were somehow so immediate.[6]

For women, all the physical work required to create bodies and keep them alive is often "so immediate." It is hard, and sometimes even impossible, for a woman to separate herself from the pressing demands of physical bodies long enough to reach the spiritual realm where quiet, contemplative communion with God is often found.

This is why God often comes down off the mountain to be with women where they are. He meets us in our kitchens, in our cars, in the street, and in our daily work. He sees the burdens we carry and knows the desires of our hearts to be with Him, and when we can't go to Him, He comes to us. Significant spiritual experiences don't always have to be received on the mountaintop. Sometimes they come to us in the most common and unexpected of places.

Thy Faith Hath Made Thee Whole

Two stories in the scriptures illustrate different ways that God speaks with us: the story of Enos in the Book of Mormon and the woman with the issue of blood in the New Testament. These stories are very different, but both show us that if our souls are truly seeking and desiring communion with God, we will find Him, no matter our situation.

In the Book of Mormon we read about Enos, who, while hunting in the woods for food for his family, found the quiet solitude he needed to pray to God. Enos tells us that his soul "hungered" and he cried unto God "in mighty prayer and supplication for my own soul, all the day long . . . and when night came I did still raise my voice high that it reached the heavens" (Enos 1:4). In response to his prayer Enos heard the voice of the Lord telling him that his sins were forgiven. When he inquired about how this was done, the Lord told him it was "because of thy faith in Christ . . . wherefore, go to, thy faith hath made thee whole" (1:8).

Interestingly, these words spoken to Enos are almost identical to the words Christ spoke to the woman with the issue of blood in the New Testament who, after twelve years of suffering from unstoppable feminine bleeding that no physician could cure, was desperate for relief. She saw Christ walking on the street and, after pushing her way through the crowd, was healed when she reached out and touched the hem of His garment. Despite the throng of people, Christ felt her touch and the power that had flowed into her. When she saw that she could not hide, the woman stepped forward and spoke with Christ. Jesus told her, "Daughter, thy faith hath made thee whole; go in peace, and be whole" (Mark 5:34). Like Enos, the woman with the issue of blood had also received the healing she was hungering after, but she received it in a very different way and in a very different place.

For the woman with the issue of blood, quiet solitude with Jesus was impossible. Due to her prolonged feminine bleeding she was unable to enter holy places, like the temple or the synagogues, where Jesus often taught. The only possible way she could reach Him was when He was out in public, and when He was in public He was always surrounded by a crowd. Since it was the only chance she had, she reached out to Him on the street, surrounded by people. This could not be any more different from Enos, who reached out to God in prayer in the solitude of the woods, but it didn't matter. She found access to God, even in a noisy and very public place.

Wrestle with God

The woman with the issue of blood and Enos both wrestled with unanswered questions, one for a whole day and night upon his knees, the other for twelve years of anguish and separation. They both experienced struggle, and both hungered for what only Christ could give them. This hunger prompted them to reach out to God, one with his heart, the other with her hand. Yet while Enos prayed, "wrestling" before God for a whole day and night to receive his answer, the woman with the issue of blood's answer came instantaneously; she was healed the very moment she reached out and touched Christ.

Why? Why were the experiences of Enos and the woman with the issue of blood so different, and yet the results were exactly the same? I think it is because God understands our circumstances and limitations. He knows that sometimes, like Enos, we *need* to slow down our lives, reevaluate our priorities, and seek Him in solace and peace. He is waiting for us to put aside our distractions and climb the mountain to speak with Him. Yet, He also knows that other times we are like the woman with the issue of blood and all we have is one moment on a crowded street, with people pressing in on us from all sides. Yet it doesn't matter if we have all the time in the world or none; one moment of faith is all it takes. If we are truly hungering and thirsting for divine communication, reaching out with all that we have, one touch, one moment, is enough.

In college I had an experience that helped me understand how we can be healed and receive answers in a moment. I had been struggling for several months with terrible, immoral thoughts. I felt like my mind had been taken over by an evil influence that constantly bombarded me with thoughts and feelings I did not want. My parents had recently gone through a divorce, and Satan must have known I was in a vulnerable spiritual state. He was waging a war for my mind and spirit. For months I begged God to make the thoughts go away or to at least be able to get some control over them, but nothing happened. I felt like Job in the Old Testament, abandoned by God and helpless against the adversary.

Then one day as I was walking across campus, jostling through throngs of students on my way home, I offered up what must have been my millionth silent prayer, begging God to heal me, to take away the torture. I'm not sure why this prayer was different, but I do know that in the middle of a crowded street, with cars zooming past and people pressing around me, God heard my prayer. He spoke to me and told me exactly what I needed to do to be healed. I did what He told me, and after months of struggle I was, almost instantaneously, able to get control over the terrible thoughts in my head. It was my own personal miracle. Like the woman with the issue of blood I had reached out to God in faith, and He healed me, even in an unexpected and crowded place.

The Power of Separation

Significantly, both Enos and the woman with the issue of blood received their special experience with God because they were separated. Enos was in the wilderness alone, separated physically from his family and his people. This distance gave him the ability to think, ponder, and pray. The woman with the issue of blood, while very much *not* physically alone, was also separated—spiritually.

In biblical times Jewish women were considered unclean during their menstrual cycles. This did not mean that they were seen as dirty or contaminated, but by having contact with blood (the source of life) they had been in contact with death and were in a state of separation from others and God until the death they had been in contact with had been atoned for through immersion in a special bath called a "mikvah."

In Hebrew, this state of separation is called "niddah" and is often a uniquely feminine situation.[7] A woman's separation lasted for as long as she was bleeding and then seven days after she was finished bleeding. For a woman with a normal cycle, this might mean a separation of a week and a half or two weeks. Yet for a woman like the woman with the issue of blood, who had continuous bleeding, it meant that she could go years without ever being able to get out of the state of being "niddah." She was forever separated from God, not because of sin but simply because of her female body.

Women, by very nature of their female bodies, have a different physical experience upon the earth than men do. There are things that happen to a woman that a man has no way of understanding. As my husband lightheartedly exclaimed once when I tried to explain to him what it felt like to have menstrual cramps, "I'm never going to understand. I don't even have that organ!"

Today women can still experience this separation from holy places due to their female bodies and female stewardships. Examples include a young woman who might not feel comfortable participating in baptisms for the dead because she is menstruating, a pregnant woman on bed rest who is unable to attend church and take the sacrament for several months, a new mother who cannot leave her breastfeeding baby to attend the temple, a woman suffering from postpartum depression who is not able to feel the Spirit like she normally does, a mother who misses all of church because she is in the foyer with a fussy toddler, a woman struggling with infertility for whom church and its emphasis on motherhood is painful, and even a menopausal woman whose hormonal changes make participating in public worship difficult. Our female bodies are beautiful, powerful, and the wellspring from which life flows, but they can also be a challenge. Like the woman with the issue of blood, sometimes there is nothing we can do to change our situation; we are just "niddah," separated because of our femaleness. And God knows this.

This is why the story of the woman with the issue of blood is so powerful. In her state of separation, a unique feminine separation, she reached out to God and found Him and accessed His power. The scriptures tell us that Jesus felt the "virtue" go out of Him when she touched Him. In Greek the word "virtue" means "soul power" or the "power a person or things exerts and puts forth."[8] In the 1828 Webster's dictionary the first definition of the word "virtue" is "strength" and refers to strength that comes from "straining, stretching and expanding." The example given with the definition has to do with plants and how the "virtue" of a plant in medicine is the power that it develops inside of itself, which can be extracted and used to heal or influence other things.

I love this definition of virtue because it helps expand our understanding of what happened when this woman reached out and touched Jesus. Not only did she access His virtue, Christ's soul power, but she also exercised her own virtue, the power she had gained through struggle, straining, stretching, and expanding. And when she touched Jesus Christ those two powers combined and brought forth a miracle.

At times we, like the woman with the issue of blood, find ourselves separated from God and from others because of our trials and sufferings. Yet those times of separateness can, just like times when we physically separate ourselves from others by going into the wilderness, be times of deep spiritual growth and communion with God. When we have deep grief or difficult questions that separate us, we begin to realize that the only one who can help us is Jesus Christ. They are times when we *must* struggle, strain, stretch and expand; times when we develop "soul power." We learn to reach out to Him, and like the woman with the issue of blood, we find that no matter where we are, He is always within our reach.

Standing with Holy Feet

Several years ago, after a particularly beautiful experience in the temple, I felt sad when it came time to change out of my white temple clothes and put on my ordinary dress and shoes. For a moment I had the crazy desire to just stay in my white clothes, to go home dressed as I was. Yet, reality quickly hit and I remembered that white clothes wouldn't stand a chance against the onslaught of food stains, baby drool, dirt from tiny hands, and other unidentifiable substances that were sure to assault them as soon as I stepped in the door of my house. The only reason my temple clothes stayed so white was that I kept them separate, saved in a special place and a special bag for a special time. I couldn't live in them all the time.

As I bent down to put my street shoes on, I was surprised to hear a scripture from Isaiah flow into my mind: "How beautiful upon the mountains are the feet of him that bringeth good tidings, that publisheth peace" (Isaiah 52:7). I looked down at my dirty brown shoes and had a beautiful feeling come over me. I realized I had just spent time standing in the temple, the mountain of the Lord, and that my feet had become holy. And if my feet were holy, then no matter where I stood, whether it be in my home, the grocery store, or church, I would be standing on holy ground.

Standing with holy feet has become a powerful image for me, and I've realized that while mountaintop experiences are important and vital to our spiritual growth, it is impossible to live on the mountain all the time. At some point we have to come down into the valley of daily work and reality. Yet with feet made holy, we can take the temple with us and everything we do becomes holy, whether it is serving in the Church, serving our neighbors, or serving dinner to our families. Our daily work can be holy work.

I have a friend whose motto is "Still Waters" because she says that no matter how chaotic things are on the surface, if you dive deep enough you will always find peaceful, still water. Sometimes finding the peace and quiet we need to hear the voice of the Lord is just a matter of diving deeper, diving into our hearts and our souls; to find ways to make our minds calm and carve out places of "separateness" where God can speak to us.

This might mean we get a babysitter, cancel appointments, and leave behind a messy house to make the trek into the mountains. Other times it may simply mean doing what we do every day—dishes, folding laundry, driving to work, vacuuming, cooking dinner, caring for others—but doing it without screens in our faces and the noise of the world in our ears; doing our work with our hearts and minds open to speaking with God. Sister Patricia Holland wrote,

> Somewhere in our lives there must be time and room for such personal communication. Somewhere in our lives there must be time and room for the celestial realities we say we believe in . . . God can only enter our realm at our invitation. He stands at the door and knocks always, but someone has to hear that knock and let him enter. In this effort we should do whatever we can to make our houses . . . the temples, quite literally, that God intends them to be.[9]

Finding ways to open the door and let God into our life can happen at any time, any place. One of my friends no longer owns a dishwasher because, as she laughingly told me, washing dishes by hand saves her a lot of money because it is good therapy for her. When life is crazy around her, the repetitive process of washing, scrubbing, and drying dishes gives her mind a calm and peaceful place to go. She says that some of her most important conversations with God have happened at her kitchen sink.

Another woman shared with me how, after coming home from work one night exhausted, she was met with the heavy burden of caring for a young son, her aging mother, and an adult daughter suffering from depression. Her house was chaotic, and her mind wasn't much clearer. She tried praying for peace but found her troubles pressed too heavily on her heart. In an attempt to bring order to her chaos, she began vacuuming and was surprised when about five minutes later she no longer felt despair. The Lord softened her heart and blessed her with a feeling of love for her family. In those few minutes of repetitive work this woman was able to find a quiet place, a place of separation. Even among the chaos God was able to speak to her.

One of the most incredible stories about God speaking to a woman while she was doing her everyday work is Mary Whitmer, one of the early matriarchs of the restored gospel. Due to persecution, the Prophet Joseph Smith, his wife Emma, and Oliver Cowdery moved from New York to Pennsylvania, into the home of Peter Whitmer. Even though they had never met Joseph and Emma before, Peter and his wife, Mary, welcomed them warmly. They provided Joseph and Oliver with a quiet place in which to complete the translation of the Book of Mormon. Mary had faith in Joseph's work, but she had eight children and the new house guests added to the burden of her work. The book *Saints: The Standard of Truth* tells how one day, while she was going about her daily chores, Mary received a witness that God was aware of her and appreciated the sacrifices she was making.

> Mary had little time to relax herself, and the added work and the strain placed on her were hard to bear. One day, while she was out by the barn where the cows were milked, she saw a gray-haired man with a knapsack slung across his shoulder. His sudden appearance frightened her, but as he approached, he spoke to her in a kind voice that set her at ease.
>
> "My name is Moroni," he said. "You have become pretty tired with all the extra work you have to do." He swung the knapsack off his shoulder, and Mary watched as he started to untie it.
>
> "You have been very faithful and diligent in your labors," he continued. "It is proper, therefore, that you should receive a witness that your faith may be strengthened."
>
> Moroni opened his knapsack and removed the gold plates. He held them in front of her and turned their pages so she could see the writings on them. After he turned the last page, he urged her to be patient and faithful as she carried the extra burden a little longer. He promised she would be blessed for it.
>
> The old man vanished a moment later, leaving Mary alone. She still had work to do, but that no longer troubled her.[10]

God had seen Mary's burden. He knew that she had a houseful of people and that she probably did not have much time or space for quiet reflection. Yet, He also knew that she was struggling and that she needed a confirmation that what she was doing, and the sacrifices she was making to enable Joseph to complete the translation of the Book of Mormon, were important and valued by God. So, in a rare, quiet moment in the barn, God sent her a divine manifestation of His love and appreciation for her work.

Like Mary Whitmer, we don't always need to be in the perfect frame of mind or the perfect place to receive revelation from God. In fact, if we only ever rely on the mountaintop experience for our spiritual growth, we may find ourselves feeling starved and hungry. Yet if we are constantly looking and listening for daily spiritual experiences, ones that come to us in the daily work of our lives, then we will find ourselves overflowing with spiritual experiences that keep our souls fed.

The story of the woman with the issue of blood reminds us that when we feel separated from God, when we may not be able to climb the mountain due to the physical demands and constraints of our life, He is there, waiting with His endless supply of strength, for us to reach out and touch Him. He knows the desires of our hearts, and if we are reaching, stretching, and straining toward Him, it only takes one touch, one moment to fill ourselves with His power, to heal our bodies, our hearts, and our homes.

A Treasured Friendship

by Jen Mabray

"Ye are my friends."

—JOHN 15:15

*O*n one of the last nights of His mortal life, sitting at a prepared feast, Jesus spoke with His disciples and said, "Ye are my friends . . . for all things that I have heard of my Father I have made known unto you. Ye have not chosen me, but I have chosen you" (selections from John 15:14–16). Once when reading this scripture, I recorded my own response to Jesus in my scripture journal: *I am your friend, too.*

I believe God deeply desires to have a friendship with us. Some might worry that seeking a companionship with God sounds too casual or trivial, and it is true that we need to avoid becoming over-familiar and irreverent in our relationship with Him. Although I believe we must always respect and reverence the eternal and devoted roles of the Divine, I also believe we can and should desire a face-to-face friendship with God, even a genuine friendship knit together from a lifetime of shared experiences. My husband once shared that he felt the closer we connect with God through communication and friendship, the more we actually grow to reverence and respect Him.

What do you think it means to have a close friendship with Jesus? I imagine on the streets of Palestine two thousand years ago, the mortal Jesus laughed and told jokes, had favorite foods and dined with friends, helped a neighbor move something heavy, joined in a game of sport with a group of gathered children, listened intently when a friend was in need, and wept with loved ones during experiences of sorrow and difficult sadness. I believe our Lord is the same today as He was then.

In my early twenties during the difficult time of my parents' divorce, I had a dream that Jesus came to my home. It was just the two of us. I do not recall what He said to me, but I remember I felt loved and happy, and had a deep admiration and devotion to Him. Somehow, He felt familiar to me, like we had been friends for a long time. His countenance was beautiful, peaceful, and held my complete attention. A bird flew in from an open window, perched on His hand, and stared up at Him. He seemed to know of my love for birds and lifted His hand to mine. The bird jumped to my finger and chirped at me. When it was time for Jesus to leave, the bird flew off my finger and followed Him.

On occasion I daydream and recall the imagery of that dream. Through my own experiences and the stories of others I have grown to have complete confidence that God seeks a friendship with us—all of us. God comes to us when we hunger for spiritual connection, during times of great distress— even trauma—during joyous occasions and celebrations, during the dawn and dusks of life, and most especially during ordinary moments. If we learn to recognize when God is near, no doubt we will knit a beautiful and life-long relationship with Him, even a woven tapestry of memories.

Connection with God

Our hearts long to be connected to our Divine Family. We want to cultivate special experiences with them. As women, I believe we are uniquely designed to wield and value connection and intimate relation-ships with each other and with God. In Deuteronomy, the Lord instituted this commandment, "Love the Lord your God with all your heart and with all your soul and with all your strength" (Deuteronomy 6:5). Per-haps this verse is more telling about the depth of God's love for us—a complete, whole, and eternal love. If we follow His commandment to do the same, He knows it will develop in us relationships that personify His love. When I imagine women having a relationship with God, I see us having vibrant conversations, sharing our thoughts and emotions, feeling peaceful trust, having purposeful gatherings, and never tiring of one-on-one, soul-reaching moments. I feel, since Eve first walked the earth, God has desired a close relationship with each of His daughters.

Jesus exemplified this kind of relationship with women in His mortal life. There is little doubt that many unrecorded experiences and special moments happened between Jesus and women. In Jesus' mortal life, many traditional and cultural boundaries prevented women from having formal experiences with God. In addition, cultural tradition prohibited women from traveling with, speaking with, or sitting at the feet of a rabbi, and rabbinical directives counseled against teaching a woman scripture.[11] Tradition and cultural boundaries are man-made, and although not inherently evil, both often encompass biases, ignorance, and prejudices regarding gender and social justice. Unfortunately, some traditions have contributed to the abuse of women, controversy and oppression of gender, sexual violation, and sadly an imbalance of women's voices and experiences throughout scripture.

Tradition is not scripture. Paul tells us in 2 Timothy 3:16, "All scripture is given by inspiration of God, and is profitable for doctrine, for reproof, for correction, for instruction in righteousness." What does *scripture* say about women? More important, what does God think about women in inspired scripture? Who are we to Him? If we return to the scriptures as Paul counseled, more often than not, we have to read through a messy backdrop of prevailing and pervasive traditional barriers that push women to the background of the text, behind the religious elite. Jesus championed women and womanhood, visited them, healed them, and often broke cultural norms between women and the religious elite. Among some cultural norms that Jesus broke, we are told iconic women like Mary Magdalene, Joanna, and Susanna traveled safely with Jesus. They traveled without refute with a known rabbi. Can you imagine the bond they developed during those travels? In addition to traveling companions, some women like Salome, Mary the mother of James and Joses, and Mary and Martha, supported Jesus' ministry using their personal resources.[12] We are told of Jesus' feelings for Mary and Martha in an insightful passage: "Jesus loved Martha, and her sister" (John 11:5). They also loved Him and opened their homes to host Him and His followers, and engaged with Him at parties, gatherings, and intimate social settings. I like to think His female friends were considered among His beloved and treasured companions.

In His time, Jesus broke through many cultural norms and *came* to women. He allowed women to embrace Him, touch Him, travel with Him, minister with Him, learn from Him, and be firsthand recipients of His compassion, love, kindness, respect, forgiveness, and doctrines. Thankfully and beautifully, Jesus' actions are embedded in scripture as the word of God. Written and whispered inspirations, feelings, and experiences between God and women, from antiquity throughout modernity, teach us that His love and holy affection for us is a pattern that started in the beginning and has never ceased. All women, no matter what corner of the earth we occupy, no matter our station in life, no matter our educational background, no matter the hour of our lives, are beloved and treasured by God. Elder James E. Talmage of the Quorum of the Twelve Apostles taught, "The world's greatest champion of woman and womanhood is Jesus the Christ."[13]

A Beautiful Relationship

When I consider the prominent friends in Jesus' mortal life, Mary and Martha always make the list. I picture the two women as some of His beloved and devoted friends, with a relationship built upon trust, love, honest expression, open communication, and familiarity. One of my favorite themes of Mary and Martha's relationship with Jesus is the fact that during His ministry, they were not treated as second-class citizens. Jesus championed women and womanhood. He recognized Mary and Martha with full rights to receive His instruction. In a few extraordinary accounts of Jesus and Mary and Martha, we see Jesus break cultural norms, and we can deduce that God seeks to have a special and holy relationship with women. He invites women, collectively and individually, to be in His circle. It's up to us.

By the time Mary and Martha's names appeared in the Gospels, Jesus had reached what we might define as celebrity status today. He had already fed the five thousand, and the Pharisees were watching His actions. Rumors of Him circulated throughout Judea and the surrounding regions (see Luke 7:17). The more He petitioned those He had healed to tell no one, the more His whereabouts and actions were published (see Mark 7:36). Peter tells us that people thronged and pressed Jesus in the streets for healing (see Luke 8:45). On occasion, His disciples had to secure a separate exit when His teachings and actions excited individuals to anger against Him, like when an angry mob from Nazareth, also the town associated with His identity, grabbed Him and tried to throw Him off the cliff side of their city (see Luke 4:29). Celebrities today have shared their difficulties to find and retain true friends who want neither a hand-out or fame. It is likely Jesus' beloved friends were a small group; however, I cannot imagine Him refusing anyone who wanted to have a relationship with Him.

Martha, Mary, and their brother Lazarus lived in Bethany, about two miles outside of Jerusalem on the southeastern slope of the Mount of Olives. Their friendship with Jesus was such that He felt comfortable enough to stop by for meals. To a would-be follower He once explained, "Foxes have holes, birds have nests, but the son of man hath no where to lay his head" (Luke 9:58). Elder Jeffrey R. Holland interpreted that verse to mean "at some point in His adult life, our Lord was homeless."[14] Humble as His circumstances may have been, it seems that He knew He could count on the open arms and hospitality of Martha when He was near her home. He knew Martha would graciously receive Him. No doubt she knew He almost always came with a crowd, many of them hungry men, but she could and was willing to handle it.

On one occasion, when Jesus came into Bethany, Martha graciously hosted: "Now it came to pass, as they went, that he entered into a certain village: and a certain woman named Martha received him into her house" (Luke 10:38–42). Because the text says, "He was received into her house," it is necessary to consider this was a quiet meal between Jesus and His two beloved friends, making the exchange between the three a very special and intimate gathering. It is also possible the occasion was a larger gathering of friends, families, disciples, and followers. Alfred Edersheim (1825–1889, France), a biblical scholar and Jewish convert to Christianity, suggests this was the holy time of Sukkot, or Feast of Tabernacles.[15] Sukkot is a biblically commanded seven-day festival in the fall, from Leviticus 23, wherein Jews gather, often in large groups of friends and families, to celebrate God and each other in a flimsy booth-like structure that serves as a reminder of the hardships of the Israelite sojourn in the wilderness and their redemption from Egypt. Edersheim studied the Gospels to produce what he felt was a correct chronological timeline of the journeys of Jesus Christ and believed Jesus was traveling up to Jerusalem during the time of Sukkot and tarried in Bethany with Mary and Martha.[16] If indeed it was the Feast of Tabernacles, Martha and her household likely would have constructed an outdoor *Sukkah*, a hut-like structure with three sides wrapped in palm or olive leaf-type foliage and a purposely poorly thatched roof so any gathered family and friends could see the stars and hear the word of God.[17] Jews still celebrate Sukkot today in a *Sukkah*, during a week-long celebration of sharing and fellowship.

In Fall 2020, after Yom Kippur, my Hebrew professor arranged for our classes to be held outside in a large *Sukkah*. A ritual lulav (a closed frond of a palm branch woven together with two willow and three myrtle branches) and etrog (citrus) were placed on the table, and all of my Jewish cohorts took turns shaking the lulav and then reciting the traditional Hebrew blessing. Fresh fruits and veggies were in abundance for lunch, and my fellow cohorts asked if I wanted to join the supper feast, which included an enormous amount of breads, cakes, dumplings, fruits, pastas, and veggies. Singing, prayers, blessings, and learning certain portions of Torah occupied the feast. If Jesus attended a portion of the Feast of Tabernacles at Martha's home, this would have been a huge honor for her household. She probably knew Jesus well enough to know His favorite foods, and it is likely that no expense or detail was spared in her preparation for the most holy guest she would ever host, the Master Teacher, Jesus the Christ.

The narrative then explains, "And she had a sister called Mary, which also sat at Jesus' feet and heard his word" (Luke 10:39). Often when this story is read, Mary is favored over her sister Martha for her decision to sit at the feet of the Master. Evelyn T. Marshall, who wrote in the January, 1987 *Ensign* magazine, said, "For years I have mistakenly assumed that Mary sat at Jesus' feet while Martha worked in the kitchen. Not so. In verse 39, Luke carefully explains that 'Martha had a sister named Mary, which *also* sat at Jesus' feet, and heard his word'" (Luke 10:39, italics added).[18] According to this view, Mary *and* Martha sat at His feet.

In my own view, although Martha may not have sat at His feet during that specific hosting occasion, the word *also* means that she was accustomed to doing so. Jesus and Martha were friends. She loved Him. A universal trait of friendship is listening to one another. Even though some might be accustomed to attributing the word *also* only to Mary's actions, I like to think the word *also* relates instead to Martha and her normal actions.

Mary and Martha Gain More Understanding

Next, we transition to the familiar domestic squabble between Mary and Martha. Instead of helping Martha serve, Mary listened to Jesus, and Martha was "cumbered about much serving," and approached Jesus and asked, "Lord dost thou not care that my sister hath left me to serve alone? Bid her therefore that she help me. And Jesus answered and said unto her, Martha, Martha, thou art careful and troubled about many things: But one thing is needful and Mary hath chosen that good part, which shall not be taken away from her" (Luke 10:40–42).

Martha wanted Jesus to tell Mary to help her, rather than sit and listen. A few things stand out to me in this initial exchange. First, recall the traditional prohibition in the ancient world for a woman to speak with a rabbi. That space was typically reserved for men. Mary sat in the position of a learner at the feet of Jesus, and He ignored a tightly maintained cultural boundary in this setting by not rebuking her. She wanted to hear Jesus. And so, she did. Jesus embraced Mary's decision to learn and invited Martha to do the same, perhaps as she had on other occasions. It is important to understand that women are not rebuked or refused by God. This is a beautiful example of God interacting with women through genuine friendships and mutual respect and strongly illuminates the character of God. He does not uphold traditional gender inequalities set by men. In fact, He does quite the opposite. In small glimpses throughout canonized texts, Jesus defended and elevated the status of women. He came to them and supported their desires to be learners, leaders, and ministers.

The second thing that stands out to me is Jesus never said what Martha was doing was unimportant, nor did He commission Mary to neglect any future serving duties. Often when people read this account, they associate Martha as a hard-working hostess, occupied with the details of the meal, while Jesus and any listeners engaged in some sort of discussion, perhaps in another room. Frequently among women I hear personal comparisons like, "I need to stop being a Martha and be more like a Mary," or "I am naturally like Martha. I wish I was like Mary." This line of thinking no doubt has made some women feel shame for too often choosing or needing to be busy rather than offering their undivided attention to discipleship. Jesus came to Mary and Martha and on that occasion, the most needful thing to do was to listen. Although the assumption that Jesus was there to eat is valid, it is certain that He felt Martha's growth was more important than His needs.

Recent scholarship, though, has constructed a different interpretation for Martha's "much serving." It is suggested by scholars of the New Testament that the phrase "much serving" is more closely aligned with the work or service of an ancient church deacon and their responsibilities to minister to the needs of others in the faith, which included a devotion to proclaiming God's word and daily provision for others.[19] In the book of Acts, Peter commissioned Phillip to administer to the "serving" needs of the church, not as an apostle but as a deacon (Acts 8:26–40). Since the word "serving" is also used to describe Martha's actions, from the perspective of church service, the labors of ministering and serving others actually adds to her regular "household responsibilities." If Martha was in the practice of "much serving," she may have lacked personal time for spiritual nourishment and perhaps was unaware of her own spiritual depletion. By calling her to His feet, Jesus recognized what she was neglecting for herself and did not deprive her the opportunity to listen and grow. God knows we offer so much of ourselves to our families, loved ones, friends, co-workers, neighbors, and strangers. Despite our holy work, spiritual nourishment cannot be ignored. King Benjamin in the Book of Mormon counseled not to run faster than we have strength, but to be diligent and to do all things in order (see Mosiah 4:27). Even Jesus withdrew Himself from the crowds and sought to replenish His soul through personal communion with His father in prayer (see Matthew 14:23, Mark 1:35, Mark 6:46, Luke 5:16, John 6:15). If we are to effectively minister to others, we must take time to fill our souls with spiritual sustenance.

Regardless of the differing interpretations of much serving, it is clear that according to the narration in Luke, Jesus intended for Martha to be in the position of a listener and a learner during His visit. If we turn this concept into a principle, we can deduce that when God comes to women, He desires for us opportunities to slow down, to hear Him, and to be nourished.

To help us consider that day in Bethany, I have created a textual elaboration of the phrase "much serving" and what it may have been like in Martha's time based on the few interpretations that I have touched on earlier, and ideas and details gathered from other scriptural accounts offered in the Gospels. The imagined scene below might help us to see what kept Martha from sitting still and the purpose of Jesus' visit to His dear friend.

> Mary *and* Martha both loved to sit at the feet of the Savior. He always taught them truths that filled their hearts, and unlike other teachers, He never sent them away. They found they never tired of learning His doctrines, and the way He taught invigorated their souls. They both felt a desire to tell others. After He was gone, Mary and Martha found they always hungered for more. One of the focal points of His doctrine was to serve and love one another, and in so doing, it would be like serving God. Martha was especially excited about this teaching. *I love this work!* she thought.

Martha was not expecting Jesus today, but He was coming to Bethany, and any chance she could take, she would have Jesus in her home. After all, she had already built a flimsy *Sukkah* in the courtyard in preparation for the commemoration of the Feast of Tabernacles. The structure was perfectly imperfect! Anyone who dined inside could see the stars through the roof and offer thanks to God for their blessings, just like their fathers did long ago at Sinai. *How ironic,* she thought, *that Jesus would be in my Sukkah!* She would have to work diligently, but she felt she could put a lovely meal together for the occasion and was so pleased He was there.

Cumbered by the needs to feed the growing crowd, Martha could only sit down for a few minutes here and there. *Maybe I can listen from the doorway and still get the food ready.* New guests called at the gate; they too heard Jesus was near. She graciously invited them in, inquired of their immediate needs, and then directed them to take a place and listen to her treasured friend, Jesus of Nazareth.

After sneaking away again to check the simmering food, Martha returned to sit but could only gather a few words before she smelled the perfect aroma of baked bread. She ran back to the kitchen to retrieve the loaves from the fire. A few more guests arrived, and she carefully calculated whether or not she had prepared enough food for everyone. *I love the work of ministering,* she thought. *My house is full, Jesus is here, and we are about to have a lovely meal together and learn more from Him. But where is Mary? How has she not noticed or thought to help me? Is she not my sister who lives here too? Maybe if I interrupt for just a minute, Jesus will remind her she needs to help.*

"Lord," she stammered, "there are lots of guests here now and Mary has left me alone to serve them. Can you get her attention and send her to help me?"

Jesus looked lovingly at His sweet friend. Her devotion to others set her apart from many others. In addition to caring for all those in her reach, she was always so attentive and proactive to His needs. He knew He could count on Her for anything, and He chuckled that He was now in the middle of a domestic spat. "Martha, Martha . . ." He began. "Don't you know that I purposely came to see you and Mary? Mary has already figured that out. We will not starve. You would never let that happen. And it appears that everyone is well taken care of and comfortable in your home. Come, my treasured friend. Sit here for a while and rest. Let me finish teaching. I want you to hear these things. They are important for you to know before I am gone."

Martha quickly glanced back at the half-completed table setting and looked around to notice any other needs. Yes, the food could wait, and yes it appeared all was well. His voice suddenly penetrated her many thoughts. *Martha, come and sit. I came to see you.*

If you just sit for a moment and consider the setting, can you picture a similar scene? Can you picture a loving verbal embrace from Jesus as He called her name? From this approach we see and can probably relate to the fact that Martha truly was cumbered by many things, that at least, on that day, divided her attention from His teaching. It is no different today for you and me. Our attention is pulled from Him from time to time, too.

In the April 2020 general conference, Joy D. Jones counseled, "Women wear many hats, but it is impossible, and unnecessary, to wear them all at once. The spirit helps us determine which work to focus on today."

As wives, mothers, girlfriends, and daughters, we have left our scripture study or stopped short of finishing a spiritual thought to answer the door, return a text, get back to work, finish homework, fix a meal, tend to a little one, or help a friend. How many of us have stepped out of the family room during general conference to change a diaper, stayed in the kitchen to arrange treats for the youth during a spiritual discussion, or texted a friend during sacrament meeting, wondering why they were not there? Sometimes I emotionally or mentally disengage during time intended for my spiritual growth. My mind wanders to something else I need to think about. These simple scenarios are natural and normal, but they can also divide our attention from Him. If we are constantly pulled away, it can hinder our growth potential to develop meaningful friendships with God.

My last observation of this story is that Martha may have been frustrated. To me, the fact that Martha complained to Jesus is one of the most telling facets of their relationship. She knew she could be real with the Savior of the World and tattle on her sister! It makes me laugh to imagine the setting. It seems almost silly to consider having Jesus over for a meal and complaining to Him. However, Martha shows us that sharing our frustrations with Him is a vital part of our communication and a relationship with Him. Beautifully, Martha teaches us not to fear the ugly side of our true feelings. She teaches us that we will not be rejected by Him when we are frustrated and need to complain. When we are visited by the Lord, sometimes we are not feeling optimistic and chipper about our situations, and that's okay. I love that Martha was in essence comfortable enough to tattle on Mary to Jesus and in turn was heard by Jesus.

During the first several months of the 2020 COVID-19 pandemic, I grew more and more frustrated with my husband, Todd. Like most families, we tried to figure out how to function in our temporary, perhaps not temporary, new normal. Seemingly overnight, he started to leave things out or unfinished. We share chores in our household, and my husband abandoned almost any chore half-finished. I would find the dishwasher open and half-emptied, a half-clean kitchen, cabinets left open, and groceries half-put away. Additionally, I picked up his shoes, jackets, tools, and laundry from all over the house. One morning, I found he had left his car door wide open all night, only to find a dead battery. A few times, he had killed a bug and left the smashed carcass on the floor. During this time, he also decided it would be nice to begin a new hobby of woodworking. After running the saw and sander, he would come inside and sit on the sofa, complete with wood shavings and sawdust flaking off of him, leaving a trail wherever he went. Mind you, this was *not* his normal behavior. After about a month I was literally going nuts. I could not keep up with the messes, and when I tried to talk to him about it, he became impatient with me.

Unsure of who to talk to for fear of bashing my husband to my friends, I decided I could only talk to the Lord. I am chuckling as I write this story into a book for everyone to read, when in the moment, I did not want to talk about it to anyone! I knelt in prayer and tattled everything I could recall to the Lord. I was annoyed with his sudden change of behavior and attitude and wondered where it all came from. I did not understand why he could not see that everywhere he went, he left a mess, and worse, he did not seem to care! What happened to my clean husband?

Now, I know what you are thinking. *Jen, pull yourself together! These issues are no big deal!* As I told the Lord in tears that I was tired of cleaning up after my husband, and not sure if I could handle the mess any longer, I distinctly remember the Lord communicating to me that I should consider what I am grateful for about my husband. That very night, I initiated another conversation with Todd and began describing all the messes and how I was feeling disrespected and overwhelmed by his sudden change. He was calm, but I was feeling anxious and ready to defend my position. Without telling him I had tattled to the Lord about the whole episode, he apologized and started to tell me all the things he was grateful for about *me!* He shared that since COVID hit and our kids were all sent home to do school online, he was running from one thing to the next and felt he had no time to finish any task. Since I am also a student, he did not want to pull me away from my studies to have me help. He assured me he would make a change, held me close, and told me he loved me. I was in tears. In just a moment's time, Todd melted away my hurt and reminded me of who he really was. Suddenly the assignment given to me from the Lord to be grateful acted as a healing balm for my soul, and I realized I was focused on the negative aspect of our situation and did not notice perhaps *why* Todd continued to leave things unfinished. Before I fell asleep, the most famous line in the Mary and Martha story came to mind: "Mary hath chosen that good part" (Luke 10:42). Todd was like Mary, who had chosen the better part, and I was like Martha, who tattled to the Lord. Knowing I had pulled the Lord into our little situation, I felt it was appropriate for one more prayer. I thanked Him for hearing my frustrations and explained the outcome. Both Todd and I were lifted that night after our squabble. I like to think when Mary and Martha had their squabble, the Lord's counsel helped to lift them too.

In a few cherished passages of the New Testament, we see the depth of Mary and Martha's friendship with Jesus. He comes to them, dines with them, attends to their needs, and is moved by their feelings. All the while, He never misses an opportunity to continue to pour into their hearts His gospel. Their story of face-to-face communication and expression is plain and simple, pure and relatable.

The story of Mary and Martha helps us to see that when we are visited by Him during the busyness of our lives, we must also set aside a space to give Him our undivided attention. It is not always a matter of better organization of our time, but a matter of recognizing when it is time to fill our cup with experiences with God that He stands ready and willing to offer. God not only desires us to give our time to Him, but He desires to give some of *His* time to us. He wants us to have a relationship, a close friendship, with Him.

Seeing God

by Heather Farrell

*"Blessed are the pure in heart,
for they shall see God."*

—MATHEW 5:8

In college I had a wonderful bishop. He was devoted to the scriptures, and his enthusiasm for them lit a fire inside of me that has never been quenched. During one of our conversations he asked me a question that impressed me deeply. "Heather," he said, placing his well-worn set of scriptures on the desk between us, "if you knew that all it took to unlock the heavens and see the face of God was 10,000 hours of studying your scriptures, would you do it?" He asked the question like he already knew the answer; that he could bear testimony that such devotion did indeed open the heavens.

In the years since this conversation, I have read my scriptures diligently and have realized that the deep longing of my heart is to have exactly what my college bishop described happen, to unlock the heavens and see the face of God. Yet several years ago, I began to feel discouraged because it seemed like it was only men in the scriptures who had seen the face of God. Men like Moses, Abraham, Enoch, Isaiah, Nephi, the brother of Jared, and Joseph Smith had stood in His presence and spoken with Him.[20] Where were the stories of women who had seen and spoken with God? Were there any? And if there weren't any, what did that mean for me?

Then one day I read the story of Hagar in the Old Testament. It was a story I had studied many times before, but this time I saw it with new eyes. I realized that Hagar had not only been seen *by* God in her time of difficulty, but that she had also *seen* God. Like the great prophets she, a humble servant, had spoken with the Creator of the universe face to face.

This discovery electrified my soul, and I began to look more closely at the stories of women in the scriptures. I discovered that there were other examples of women who had seen and spoken with God: Eve, Mary, Rebekah, Miriam, the mother of Samson, Hagar, the Jaredite women of the Book of Mormon, and others. These were women who had the heavens opened to them, women who had seen and spoken with God. I want to share a few of these women's stories with you to help you see that God is the same "yesterday, and today and for ever" (Hebrews 13:8) and that if He appeared and spoke to women anciently, He can appear and speak with *you*.

Hagar

The story of Hagar, the second wife of the prophet Abraham, is told in Genesis 16. We read how, after years of being childless, Sarah gave her handmaiden Hagar to Abraham to be his wife. Sarah's reason for doing this was very clear: so that "I may obtain children by her" (verse 2). Sarah, Hagar, and Abraham were entering into an ancient form of surrogacy where, by being intimate with her husband, Hagar would become pregnant with a child that would then legally become Sarah's child.

We get no indication that Hagar was forced or coerced into this agreement, but we do see that after Hagar became pregnant, the situation between Sarah and Hagar changed. Genesis 16:4 says that Sarah became "despised in her [Hagar's] eyes." In Hebrew this phrase can also be translated as Sarah was "lowered in [Hagar's] esteem," and some Jewish rabbis[21] speculate that when Hagar saw how easy it had been for her to conceive she took it as a sign that Sarah must be cursed and hated by God and that she, Hagar, was the beloved and chosen one. It is also possible that Hagar, after realizing she was pregnant, may have simply changed her mind about wanting to give her baby to Sarah.

We really don't know what transpired between these two women, but we do know that circumstances eventually became so bad that Hagar decided to run away. She fled into the wilderness of Shur: a vast, hard deseret which today is the upper part of Saudi Arabia. Even though the scriptural text gives us no indication that Hagar was traveling with other people, it would have been highly unusual and very unsafe for Hagar (a lone pregnant woman) to have made such a long trek by herself. It is more feasible that Hagar, who was Egyptian, had joined a caravan that was crossing the wilderness of Shur on its way to Egypt. She had decided to go home.

It was here in the wilderness, beside a well of water, that "the angel of the Lord found her" (verse 7). This is the part of the story that, for so many years, I overlooked. I assumed that it was simply "*an* angel *sent* by the Lord" who spoke to Hagar, but on closer study I realized that this isn't what the scripture says. It says she was found by "*the* angel of the Lord." The article "the" in front of this phrase is important, because it tells us that we are not dealing with any ordinary angel, but the one, the only, angel of the Lord.[22]

The Angel of the Lord

In Hebrew the word "angel" means "one who is sent," and while it can refer to mortal and heavenly messengers, it also refers to what scholars call the "theophanic angel." "Theophanic" is an academic word meaning the manifestation of deity in a visible way' and refers to the times in the scriptures when God reveals Himself to mortals in a way that enables them to stand in his presence and speak with Him.[23]

The best explanation of a theophanic revelation was given in Ether 3 to the brother of Jared, who, after seeing the finger of the Lord, was the first person on earth to whom Christ revealed Himself. Christ explained to Jared, "Behold, this body, which ye now behold, is the body of my spirit; and man have I created after the body of my spirit; and even as I appear unto thee to be in the spirit will I appear unto my people in the flesh" (verse 16). Christ had not yet come to the earth and had not yet gained His physical body, so He appeared to the brother of Jared in the "body of his spirit," or as the Old Testament would say it, as "the angel of the Lord."

Interestingly, this same phrase "the angel of the Lord" is used to describe the interaction that Moses had with God at the burning bush on Mount Horeb. Exodus 3 tells us that while Moses was tending his flocks, "*the* angel of the Lord appeared unto him in a flame of fire out of the midst of a bush. . . . And Moses hid his face; for he was afraid to look upon the face of God" (verses 2, 6). Moses then spoke with the Lord, receiving direction about what he was to do to free the children of Israel from bondage. When this interaction was over, Moses fell to the ground and described what had happened to him: "But now mine own eyes have beheld God; but not my natural but my spiritual eyes, for my natural eyes could not have beheld; for I should have withered and died in his presence; but his glory was upon me; and I beheld his face, for I was transfigured before him" (Moses 1:11).

Moses' experience sounds similar to what Hagar described after her interaction with the angel of the Lord was over. She said, "Have I also looked after him that seeth me?" (Genesis 16:13), or in clearer words, "How is it that I am still able to see [which means that I am still alive] after he [God] has seen me?" Hagar realized that she had spoken with God face to face and was amazed. In fact, she even gave God a name, El-Roi, which in Hebrew means "the God who sees me."[24]

This name is powerful. It teaches us what Hagar discovered; that God sees us, that He knows our names, and that He has a plan for our life. Hagar was not in an easy situation, and God knew it. He saw her suffering and the difficulty of her situation in Abraham and Sarah's home, but He also saw more than that. He saw her future. He saw the beautiful things that awaited her and the nations that would come from the unborn son she was carrying. He saw it all and gave her just a glimpse of what lay ahead. A glimpse was all she needed, and with new resolve and strength, Hagar returned to Abraham and Sarah and bore a son named Ishmael, a name which in Hebrew means "God hears."

Eyes to See

Hagar returned home to Abraham's tent, but her interactions with God were not over. Fourteen or fifteen years later, after the miraculous birth of Isaac to Sarah, Hagar and her son, Ishmael, were sent away. The reason for this was that Ishmael was found "mocking," which in Hebrew could mean any one of these: "teasing," "flirting," or "scorning."[25] Whatever Ishmael was doing, it was enough to concern Sarah. She told Abraham to send Hagar and Ishmael away, which he did only after receiving an assurance from God that Hagar and Ishmael would be okay.

Once again, Hagar found herself in the wilderness. Yet this time things did not go quite so smoothly. She and Ishmael ran out of water, and Ishmael became very sick. Hagar, resigned to the fact that her son was going to die, laid him under the shrubs and then went a "bowshot" away (Gen. 21:16) so that she did not have to see him die. Here she "lift[ed] up her voice, and wept." In response, "*the* angel of the Lord called to Hagar out of heaven" and again calling her by name, asked her "What aileth thee?" (verse 17).

It is interesting that whenever God spoke to Hagar, He began the conversation by asking her questions. The first time God visited Hagar He asked her, "Wenst camest thou? And whither wilt thou go?" (Genesis 16:8), or in other words, "Where did you come from? And where are you going?" The second time, His question of "What aileth thee?" seems ironic. Hagar was watching her son die of thirst in the wilderness! Wasn't it obvious what the problem was? Why would God, who is omniscient, ask questions He already knows the answer to?

Author Michael Kelley wrote,

> God uses questions to force us to confront our own hearts. He questions us not because He needs to know and understand something about what's going on, but because He wants us to know and understand the truth of what's going on. Through questions, God forces us to turn our gaze on ourselves, our hearts, and our motivations. He makes us look deeply into ourselves, knowing that He already knows, and then own up to that which we have either been unable or unwilling to see previously.[26]

God uses questions to probe the depths of our hearts—to help us see and understand ourselves and our situation on earth better. He helps us discover. For example, after Adam and Eve partook of the fruit in the Garden of Eden, God called Adam by name, just like He did Hagar, and asked him, "Where art thou?" (Genesis 3:9). God knew where Adam was, but His question forced Adam and Eve to evaluate what had happened and discover where they were headed.

I think God's questions to Hagar had a similar effect. They forced her to look inward for answers, rather than outward, helping her evaluate where she had been, where she was going, and what she wanted in life. God's questions helped Hagar learn to see. The first time, His questions opened up her eyes to see that the path she was on, the one heading back to Egypt, was not the right one. She gained the courage to return to a difficult situation and to see it with new eyes. The second time, God's question, "What aileth thee?" helped her to see that in reality that there was nothing ailing her, because God had provided her with everything she needed. In Genesis 21:19 we read that "God opened up her eyes" and she discovered a well where she was able to get water to save her life and the life of her son. Everything she had needed and wanted had already been provided; she just needed eyes to see it.

We too have been given everything we need. It is all before us. All the questions and the mysteries of the universe that we long to understand, all the prosperity and peace we desire for our families and nations, and all the healing and help we need have already been provided for us. We simply need God's help to see it—to discover the well of healing, knowledge, and peace that God, who sees us and knows our burdens and struggles, has already placed in our path.

Like Hagar, God sees us—not just as we are in this one moment in time, but He sees the complete us; the person we were before we came to earth, the person we are on the earth, and the person we will be after we leave this earth. His picture of us is so big, so complete. He is the only one who truly sees us, and with His help we can learn to see who we are: yesterday, today, and forever.

Samson's Mother

The next story I want to share about a woman who saw God is one that very few people know. Her story is often overlooked because the life of her son, Samson, is so exciting and dramatic. Yet Samson's mother, whose name we unfortunately don't know, has an incredible story; one that is equally exciting as the life of her powerful son. Her experience provides us with more evidence that God appears and speaks to women in remarkable ways.

In Judges 13 we read about Samson's' mother and her husband, named Manoah, and their struggle to have a child. One day, "the angel of the Lord" (verse 3) appeared to Manoah's wife and told her that she would bear a son and that he would be a Nazarite (a person dedicated to God) from before he was born. Moreover, he would deliver the Israelite from their Philistine oppressors, something that the Israelites had been praying for but which seemed impossible because of the power and military might of the Philistine nation. The Lord also gave her instructions to "drink not wine nor strong drink, and eat not any unclean thing" (verse 4) while she was pregnant and to not cut her son's hair (which were both parts of making a Nazarite covenant) because of the special mission her son was to perform.

After this visitation, the woman went to her husband and told him about her experience. She described the person she had seen, saying, "A man of God came to me, and his countenance was like the countenance of an angel of God, very terrible; but I asked him not whence he was, neither told he me his name" (verse 6). Like Hagar, Samson's mother was visited by "*the* angel of the Lord" and not simply "an" angel. She had been in the presence of God, but did not fully comprehend what had happened to her.

After hearing of her experience, Manoah prayed to the Lord asking that the "man of God" would return and "teach us what we shall do unto the child that shall be born" (verse 8). It seems that Manoah needed his own confirmation of what his wife had said. He wanted to see and hear the message for himself. Yet, we read that "God hearkened to the voice of Manoah "but that the angel of the Lord did not come to him but came again to his wife, as she "sat in the field" (verse 9).

There are two things that I love about this. First, this woman was visited by God while she was working, doing the everyday tasks required to provide and care for her family. We read that she "sat" in her field. I can imagine her, tired and worn out after hoeing and planting, taking a break to ponder and meditate in the middle of her work. Or it might have been that this divine revelation came to her, not when she was mediating but sitting on the ground digging up vegetables or weeds. Either way, the Lord came to her where she was, in the midst of her daily work.

Second, I love that the angel came *again* to the woman and not to Manoah. This message was for her. It concerned her body and her stewardship, and so the Lord spoke directly to her. In fact, when the woman ran to get Manoah and he saw the heavenly presence for himself he asked the Lord to tell him "how we shall order the child, and how shall we do unto him?" (verse 12). In response, the angel of the Lord told him, "Of all that I said unto the woman let her beware" (verse 13) or in other words, "I already told your wife everything; she knows what she needs to do." I don't think the Lord was trying to belittle Manoah's role or importance as a father, but He was simply making it clear that His message was for the woman and that it was her revelation and her responsibility. Manoah's job was to believe and support her.

Interestingly, at this point neither Manoah nor his wife seem to fully comprehend who their messenger is. They invite Him into their house to eat, which He refuses but tells them to offer up a sacrifice instead. Manoah then asked the angel of the Lord His name, to which He replied that His name was "secret" (verse 18), which in Hebrew means "wonderful" or "incomprehensible."[27]

Significantly, this is the same word used by Isaiah when he spoke of the Messiah in Isaiah 9:6: "For unto us a child is born, unto us a son is given: and the government shall be upon his shoulder; and his name shall be called Wonderful."[28] This woman and her husband were speaking with Jehovah, Jesus Christ, and did not know it.

It wasn't until after Manoah offered up a sacrifice that a "wonderful" thing happened; the angel of the Lord ascended in the flame on the altar up into heaven. This marvelous sight overwhelmed Manoah and his wife, and they "fell on their faces to the ground" (verse 20). They finally realized that they had been in the presence of God. This knowledge terrified Manoah and he said, "We shall surely die, because we have seen God" (verse 22). Yet his wife, who seemed to have a firm grasp on what God wanted her to do, reassured him by telling him, "If the Lord pleased to kill us, he would not have . . . showed us all these things, nor would . . . have told us such things as these" (verse 23).

Like Hagar, this woman had stood in the presence of God, spoken with Him face to face, and received divine direction and revelation not only for her own life and the life of her child, but for the future of the entire Israelite nation. She knew that she was not forgotten, not abandoned, but that God knew her and had given her the ability to free her people from bondage. She was obedient to all that God told her to do and gave birth to Samson, a mighty man who later became the judge of Israel. He did exactly what the Lord had promised his mother he would do-- he delivered Israel from out of the hands of the Philistines.

Recognizing God

A common theme in the story of Hagar and Samson's mother is the idea of learning to recognize God. It wasn't until *after* their experiences with God, when they took time to reflect on them, that both Hagar and Samson's mother realized they had been in the presence of God. I think that, like these women, we may have spiritual experiences or divine manifestations in our life that we may not fully appreciate or recognize unless we have our eyes and hearts open to seeing and understanding.

I often read to my children a story called "The Rough Faced Girl" by Rafe Martin, about a Native American village in which lived the "Invisible Being." Tradition said that any girl who could see the Invisible Being could be his wife, and so all the girls in the village tried, but none were able to see him. One day, Rough Faced Girl, who had been burned and abused by her wicked sisters, decided to approach the house of the Invisible Being, hoping to become his bride. Her sisters, who had both already failed the test, laughed at her, but she was undaunted. When she approached the house of the Invisible Being, she was met by his sister, who welcomed Rough Faced Girl into the wigwam. The sister could see into the hearts of others and knew immediately there was something special and different about this girl. She began to ask Rough Faced Girl questions to see if she, unlike all the other village girls, could see her brother, the Invisible Being.

"What is my brother's bow made of?" the sister asked. Other girls had replied with common things like oak and rawhide, but Rough Faced Girl replied, "His bow is the great curve of the rainbow." The sister smiled because she knew that this girl could truly see her brother. "What is the runner of his sled made of?" the sister asked next, to which Rough Faced Girl answered, "His sled is the Milky Way of stars that spreads across the sky." The illustrations in the story are beautiful and show a face in the sky, one easily missed if you are not looking closely, made of clouds, birds, trees, and a rainbow. They show that the Invisible Being was visible the entire time, it just took humble eyes, like those of Rough Faced Girl, to see him.

In fact, when the sister took Rough Faced Girl to the wigwam of the Invisible Being, she was not surprised or afraid when he entered. She had already seen him and knew who he was. The Invisible Being saw the beauty in her soul and was honored to have her as his wife.

I love this story because it teaches a simple but powerful lesson, that God is much nearer and more visible than we realize. As God told Moses in Moses 6:63, "All things are created and made to bear record of me, both things which are temporal, and things which are spiritual; things which are in the heavens above, and things which are on the earth, and things which are in the earth, and things which are under the earth, both above and beneath: all things bear record of me."[29] We can see God every day of our life by learning to recognize Him.

Elder Henry B. Eyring shared how, over the course of many years, he learned how to recognize and see God. He said, "I wrote down a few lines every day for years. I never missed a day no matter how tired I was or how early I would have to start the next day. Before I would write, I would ponder this question: 'Have I seen the hand of God reaching out to touch us or our children or our family today?' As I kept at it, something began to happen. As I would cast my mind over the day, I would see evidence of what God had done for one of us that I had not recognized in the busy moments of the day. As that happened, and it happened often, I realized that trying to remember had allowed God to show me what He had done."[30]

In order to see God more clearly in our lives and the world around us, we need, like Elder Eyring, to take time to ponder, reflect, and express gratitude for what we have and what we have experienced. As we do this, our eyes will be opened and we will see and comprehend the enormity and majesty of God. We will see His face in the beauty of the world, in the faces of others, in the scriptures, in the prophets, and in the miracle of life.

Piercing the Cloud

The first step toward seeing and speaking with God is to believe that you can; to have faith that such an experience is possible. Studying these stories of women in the scriptures who saw and spoke to Him can strengthen our faith that such miracles can happen to us as well. Yet sometimes, no matter how much we hope and wish for miraculous experiences, we are withheld because of our own obstinate cloud of unbelief.

Interestingly, in the scriptures we have several accounts of people seeing or speaking with God "in a cloud." For example, in Numbers 12:5 it says that "the Lord came down in the pillar of the cloud" and spoke to both Aaron and Miriam, chastising them for their criticisms of Moses. Similarly, in Ether 2:4 we read how the "Lord came down and talked with the brother of Jared; and he was in a cloud, and the brother of Jared saw him not." Yet it was not just to the brother of Jared that the Lord spoke, but to all of the Jaredites. Ether 12:5 tells us that "the Lord did go before them, and did talk with *them* as he stood in a cloud." The use of the plural pronoun "them" indicates that many of the Jaredites—perhaps even their women—saw God in the cloud and spoke with Him.

For me the image of God appearing and speaking in a cloud conjures up mythological images of high mountains, where with one's head brushing the clouds, a person speaks directly to deity. So there is something beautiful and humbling about the image of that cloud, shrouding the divine presence, descending down to earth to speak and interact with people on earth—not just prophets, but ordinary people like you and me.

If God can, and does, descend to earth to talk with us, then our task becomes learning to see beyond that cloud, learning to pierce the heavens and see past the veil. For the brother of Jared, this happened only after many years of listening and following the instructions he received from the Lord. His obedience to things he could not see increased his faith until one day, when he climbed the mount to ask the Lord to give light to his stones, his faith was so great that he "could not be kept within the veil and he saw the finger of the Lord . . . for he knew, nothing doubting" (Ether 3:19).

The prophetess Anna in the New Testament has a similar story. After decades of faithful service at the temple, she was blessed to see and recognize the promised Savior when Mary and Joseph brought Him to the temple as a tiny infant. The faith and dedication of this great woman pierced the cloud of unbelief, and she saw what many others could not see. Her knowledge filled her with joy, and we read that she "spake of him [Jesus] to all them that looked for redemption in Jerusalem" (Luke 2:38).

Like Anna, God can help us see past the ordinary and view the extraordinary. He will help us learn to recognize Him in the words of the scriptures, in the words of the prophets, in the words and kind deeds of others, in the world around us, and even within our own souls. The brother of Jared's faith enabled him to see the finger of the Lord, and I know that as we exercise faith and listen to the Lord, we will be able to see the hand of the Lord reaching out to us from beyond the veil, endowing us with power, strength, and knowledge.

God is much closer and more visible that we realize. The stories of women who have seen Him, women like Hagar and Samson's mother, remind us that He sees us, that He knows our names, and that He cares about what happens to us. He wants us to be happy, and He wants us to see Him, discover Him, and have a relationship with Him.

When our first father, Adam, realized that God was not as far away as he thought, it brought him great joy. While living in the Garden of Eden, Adam and Eve had spoken openly and freely with God, but after their transgression He was veiled from them, more distant than He had been before. Yet through the process of offering sacrifices and praying, Adam and Eve learned about the Atonement and that God was not hidden from them, that He would still speak and direct them through His Son, Jesus Christ, and holy messengers. This knowledge caused Adam to proclaim, "My eyes are opened and in this life I shall have joy and again in the flesh I shall see God" (Moses 5:10). Adam knew what each of us can know, that even though we are not in His presence, God is not far from us. If our eyes are open we can have joy, and in the flesh we can—both men and women—see God.

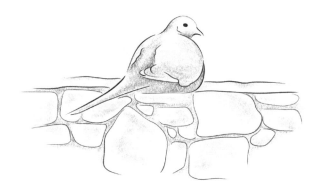

God Waits for Us

By Jen Mabray

I know that the Messiah cometh, which is called
Christ: when he is come, he will tell us all things.
Jesus said unto her, I that speak unto thee am he.

—JOHN 4:25–26

*P*ersonally, my most treasured face-to-face experience of God coming to a woman is the encounter between Jesus and the woman at the well. In the Gospel of John we read that Jesus traveled from Judaea to Galilee with His disciples and shared that He needed to go through Samaria first. He sent His disciples ahead of Him to buy food in the nearby town of Sychar while He waited at Jacob's Well. Around noon, a woman of Samaria came to draw water (see John 4:7).

Traditional commentary suggests that Jesus spoke with an outcast, a marginalized woman of ill repute, and a shamed Samaritan. Jews believed Samaritans to be ethnically mixed, theologically confused, ritually impure, and potentially dangerous due to tensions regarding biblical interpretations and geographical markers considered sacred to each group.[31] Personally, though, I have wrestled with the homily of interpretations regarding her shamed character. I am somewhat troubled by the popular belief that she was individually rejected and considered less than virtuous due to five failed marriages and her current living situation with an unmarried man, all of which were revealed by Jesus in their conversation (see John 4:17–18). Upon closer inspection, the story itself reveals the character of this woman. Despite the possibility of being truly rejected and the prominence of her life's unfairness, she seems to have religious knowledge, devotion, and a desire to worship God in the manner she felt was true.

I began to study her story again, this time from the perspective of Jewish thought and found this perspective illuminates her as a woman of strong character, devotion, even religiously educated, and ultimately in a position to testify of the Messiah, despite her many troubles. The example of Christ coming to the woman at the well teaches us that He personally seeks us. If your situation parallels or resembles the difficulties of her life, take heart. Jesus came to her and testified that He was the promised Messiah. We, too, no matter our situation, struggles, status, or position, can receive a personal witness that He is the Messiah. I believe Jesus not only rested at the well, but waited . . . for *her.*

The Significance of the Sixth Hour

We are told Jesus met with the lone woman around the sixth hour (John 4:6). The sixth hour is the noon hour or around 12 p.m. The Hebrew night ends at 6 a.m. and counts each hour into the daylight consecutively: 6 a.m. is the first hour, 7 a.m. the second hour; therefore, the sixth hour from 6 a.m. is noon.[32] Typically, women would have come to the well to fetch water in the early-morning hours. The early-morning women may have traveled in a type of watering-clan and collectively walked to and from the well together for protection, assistance, and companionship. However, what does the *sixth hour* of the day have to do with the lone woman of Samaria? Traditional commentary implies that she probably came at the sixth hour to avoid the early-morning women, either because of her questionable character or their judgmental jeers.

What if her character and objective to obtain water could be reconsidered? For example, suppose she went to the well to fetch *more* water for the second time that day. Or, maybe she wanted to be alone to obtain silence and solitude. This seems almost a silly question to ask, but when is the last time you *needed* to be alone in the middle of the day? I can almost hear the answer . . . yesterday, the day before, last week. Sometimes when I am able to have a few minutes alone, those moments are the space I need to relax, be quiet, and commune with the Lord. If the woman of Samaria needed to take some time to herself, like we all need to do from time to time, an errand to the well in the middle of the day may have been the solace she was looking for.

What if the *sixth hour* was not a strange hour to draw water? Well-watering hours were not restricted to the early morning as narrated in previous biblical accounts. For example, the daughters of Jethro, the priest of Midian (one of whom was Zipporah, who would eventually become the wife of Moses), satisfied the thirst of their father's animals in the middle of the day at the well (see Exodus 2:15–19). The biblical matriarch, Rachel, also watered her father's flock at "high day" after Jacob rolled the stone from off the mouth of the well (see Genesis 29:6–12). It is important to consider the possibility that the lone woman's errand to fetch water in the *sixth hour* was not abnormal behavior or in an effort to avoid anyone.

It is necessary, however, for us to also consider the negative aspect of the *sixth hour*. What if she really did avoid other women from her town because she felt somehow insufficient, lacking, uncomfortable, or worse—shamed? A special friend of mine gave me permission to share her story of a lengthy trial in her adult life wherein she felt she was truly lacking and insufficient, the result of which pulled her away from other women.

Nancy and her husband tried for nearly twenty years to have a baby. When no baby came, feelings of self-doubt and a lack of purpose threatened to take control of her life. Nancy witnessed the Lord's tangible power in the lives of other women who also struggled with conception, but inevitably, every woman she knew eventually had a birth story. Some women boastfully claimed they did not even have to try. Why was the righteous desire for motherhood not granted for Nancy? Was Nancy not built for motherhood, too? Nancy did as Hannah did long ago and cried out to the Lord in the "bitterness of soul" (Samuel 1:10). In a Jewish midrash, Hannah questioned the Lord, "Am I not a woman, divinely designed with a womb to carry, and breasts to sustain life?"[33] Like Hannah, Nancy prayed and fasted, and at times felt she could not handle even one more barren day.

In 2003, Nancy had a vision while she and her husband sat alone after a sacrament meeting in a chapel of The Church of Jesus Christ of Latter-day Saints. She recalled that the lights were off in the overflow section where they sat, and sunlight poured in through the windows at the front. Immediately she noticed a little girl, about four years old, playing and dancing near them on the floor. Soft blonde shoulder-length curls fluttered around her face as she danced and twirled. The girl started to run past them. Wondering where the mother of the little girl was, Nancy instinctively reached out with one arm to catch the child as she ran past, with a plan to return her to her mother. Her eyes were familiar and bright. In the instant the girl's torso should have touched Nancy's left arm, she immediately disappeared. "Did you just see that little girl?" Nancy turned and asked her husband.

"What little girl?"

"The little girl who was right here playing on the floor, with blonde hair. She ran right into my arms and disappeared!"

Nancy pondered the vision of the little girl and treasured it in her heart. As the years rolled on, though, she experienced innumerable visits to doctors and had several surgeries, but still no baby came. Her heart-wrenching situation plunged her into depression. Interaction with mothers was often the catalyst for a lengthy bout of sadness she had to work through time and time again. She sought to soothe the pain by removing herself from the company of women on Mother's Day, and during discussions centered on motherhood and new babies, and eventually grew despondent and sometimes bitter as she watched the children of her friends grow into teens and eventually become mothers of their own.

I met Nancy in 2009. She and I worked together for a time, and she confided in me one day in the kitchen at church, "I cannot handle seeing pregnant women or mothers with their growing families. It hurts too much. I plead with the Lord for answers and try to stay busy serving others, but I can't shake the depression and worthlessness I feel." Although many women were sensitive to Nancy and her feelings, she felt there was no one who could truly empathize with her, for most everyone else had children to raise. It was a blatant reminder of what she could not obtain for herself.

Like my friend Nancy, the woman at the well may have been deeply troubled in the company of other women who reminisced about babies and motherhood. For this, or any number of other reasons, she could have decided to avoid the women who would have gone to fetch water in the early morning hours. Additionally, negative social stigmas and cultural stereotypes regarding barrenness in her day could have made her feel less than other women and uncomfortable in their presence.

It is impossible to know what drew the woman to the well in the middle of the day. Her choice to go during the *sixth hour* may have been out of daily habit or a one-time errand that day. It is also possible she went to the well at that specific time because of what we might consider a spiritual prompting. Whatever her true reason, I imagine she had no idea the experience she was about to have. However, Jesus did. I think He knew she would be there and waited specifically for her.

We Are His Focus

When the woman who Jesus was waiting for arrived, He asked for a drink (John 4:7). It is likely He was thirsty, but I also think He was trying to start the conversation. Interestingly, no matter how many times I read this story, I cannot find in the text that Jesus ever actually received a drink from her. If He really was thirsty, I guess He had to conjure a way to reach the water Himself. What I really think this means is that when God comes to us, we are His focus. His timing at the well is proof that He intends to come to us, and in those given moments, we are His focus. To start the conversation, we might feel, hear, or think something that involves what we are doing at that moment, and then He begins His message. I think God nudges us with a feeling or a thought while we work through our mundane and ordinary tasks like drawing water, washing dishes, driving the car, folding laundry, cooking, cleaning the house, tending the garden, walking the dog, or really *anything* that does not completely absorb our minds and actions. Fortunately, most of these tasks are a regular part of daily life and are sometimes less consuming than our more active roles as mothers, sisters, caretakers, employees, students, managers, leaders, and disciples. Perhaps it is easier for the Lord to get our attention when we are doing our ordinary tasks.

Recently, I was alone in the kitchen washing dishes after dinner, listening to my seventeen-year-old nephew, Tyler, play the piano in the other room. He had come to stay with us for a short while. Tyler is somewhat of a prodigy when it comes to understanding the science of music, musical instruments, and composition. At fifteen, he wrote a full score for his high school marching band that took his band to state. Like I said, prodigy.

Sadly, the 2020 COVID-19 pandemic really affected his access to music. Social distancing and heightened restrictions for face-to-face interaction completely removed his opportunity to be in the band hall composing music and playing just about every band instrument possible. It was as if his voice, his creativity, and his dreams had been stolen from him. And like so many, he struggled to understand and navigate a new and uncertain normal.

My two teenage daughters adore Tyler, and the three are nearly inseparable when they are together, always deep in discussions, laughter, cooking, and playing games. He and I are also very close. I am a pianist, and our connection has always come through music. One time we sat in the car and played instrumental pieces through the speakers as loud as we could so we could hear all the different instrumental voices.

As I washed the dishes that night, I felt my heart and mind speak to me. "Leave the dishes and go be with Tyler." I stopped in the middle of rinsing a plate and contemplated what I thought I had just heard. Another thought came: "Jen, the dishes do not matter right now. Go sit with him and play."

I dried my hands and left the dirty dishes on the counter and sat at the piano bench with Tyler. His comment melted my heart. "Oh! I was hoping you would come in here! I wrote this. Can you play it?"

We sat that night for almost two hours at the piano taking turns on the keys. The next day, we went to the church building. Tyler, my two teen daughters, and I brought all our string instruments and performed before no one for more than four hours. We had access to a grand piano, an organ, a violin, and a viola. We opened everything up as loud as we could and just played. It was exhilarating! Tyler happily reminisced about those hours every day until he went home.

My experience with Tyler was simple and sweet. The result was intimately impactful and needed for both of us. Had I been intently focused on my studies for school or deep in conversation with one of my children, I may have missed His conversation starter that began with a few words about the dishes. Because I was in the middle of something more ordinary, I think I heard Him. I believe God communicates with us during our ordinary tasks because it is easier to get our attention. If we are willing to pause and allow Him to steer the conversation, not only will we feel like He is focused on us, but we may also be participants in opportunities to help others.

Water and Laws

After Jesus asked for a drink, the woman pushed back against Jesus' forwardness, no doubt restrained by societal norms. She questioned why a Jew was even speaking to her, a woman of Samaria, who by ancient tradition had no dealings with each other. Jesus countered, "If thou knewest the gift of God, and who it is that saith to thee, Give me to drink; thou wouldest have asked of him, and he would have given thee living water" (John 4:10).[34] What do you imagine was her expression at this point? Personally, her response makes me chuckle. Perhaps with one eyebrow raised and skepticism in her voice, she peered at the Jewish man and said, "Sir, thou hast nothing to draw with, and the well is deep, from whence then hast thou *that* living water?" (John 4:11, emphasis added). The story develops quickly from here, and we get to see more of her character.

She asked Jesus if He was greater than her ancient religious father Jacob, the grandson of Abraham, who gave them the well that supported their families, communities, and travelers. Jesus made a striking claim to her declaration: "Anyone who drank of Jacob's water would feel thirsty again" (John 4:13). Then he offered the promise, "But whosoever drinketh of the water that I shall give him shall never thirst; but the water that I shall give him shall be in him a well of water springing up into ever-lasting life" (John 4:14). Remember, they are in the desert. Water is life. A Jew was offering to her not just water to sustain life, but water to bring everlasting life!

How do you think she internalized the concept of *everlasting* water? How would you? My mind would quickly process that I would not have to come to the well any longer. Likely I would not have thought of any spiritual application to the phrase "living water." I marvel at her response and how her tone and original defense toward Jesus changed. "Sir, give me this water, that I thirst not, neither come hither to draw" (John 4:15). Suddenly she was not concerned that He was a Jew, or where the water came from, only that she obtained from Him this *everlasting* water. Then they hit a roadblock. Legally she could not take anything from the man Jesus, lest she be considered a "loose" woman because she interacted with a man who was not her husband. Jesus knew the cultural customs and asked her to go and get her husband.

> Jesus saith unto her, Go, call thy husband, and come hither. And the woman answered and said, I have no husband.
> Jesus said unto her, Thou has well said, I have no husband: For thou hast had five husbands; and he whom thou now hast is not thy husband. (John 4:16–18)

Jesus' ability to know everything about her must have shocked her when He shared He knew she had no husband, but that she had had five husbands and was currently living with a man who was not her husband. What type of events could have produced five prior marriages in this woman's life? Five husbands might seem slightly excessive to modern readers. It could also be a literary exaggeration to make a point. If Jesus came to a woman of Samaria who had had five husbands, and was living with a sixth man, then surely, He would come to any one of us who also have unpleasant experiences in our lives. Yet, if she really did have five husbands, let's explore what this might mean using Jewish thought. To do this, I will draw from Jewish tradition and law located in sacred texts.

The Samaritans were not Jews, but they kept or guarded a slightly altered version of Mosaic law according to the Pentateuch, the first five books of Moses.[35] According to Mosaic interpretation, it was considered a legal obligation for a man to procreate.[36] Thus, if a woman was barren, her husband had legal merit to divorce her.[37] We also learn from Deuteronomy that if a woman was found unfavorable in the eyes of her husband, he could divorce her (see Deuteronomy 24:1). Biblical law deplores divorce, but it was given to Moses as an option for the Israelites. To expound this idea, both of these legal directives mean that if the lone woman could not bear children, or if she had an unfavorable flaw, then by Mosaic law a husband could divorce her, and afterward she had no legal rights. Additionally, according to Mosaic law, legally only the man could initiate and give a bill of divorcement, called a *get* (see Deuteronomy 24:1–4), which means it's possible she never initiated divorce. Here is the tricky part, though; after a woman received one *get,* she was often labeled through tradition as ritually defiled, and thereafter had to manage difficult and degrading social stigmas in every subsequent marriage (see Deuteronomy 24:4). Her subsequent husbands probably knew of her previous marriages, which compounded any natural difficulty within the new marriage.[38] Presumably, then, we could imagine that although her divorces may not have been her doing, it might have been nearly impossible for her to find a righteous man and not be seen by others, including herself, as flawed.

Outside of Jewish law and interpretation, we need to consider the possibility that a previous husband or two could have passed away. Often a widow's reputation and story will precede her. We have women in our circles who have lived through the horrible trauma of unexpectedly losing a spouse to unexplained sudden deaths, illnesses, old age, accidents, and even suicide. Too often, women come upon the scene of their spouses' deaths and have to live with haunting images and shattered dreams. We weep when we learn these traumas. I personally know some women who have a godly capacity to mourn with those that mourn. It's a gift, really. And, there are those who have trouble contemplating the pain of another and unfortunately turn a deaf ear. There may have been both types of women, and everywhere in between, in the life of the woman at the well. From her perspective, if she had to experience the death of a husband or two, she may not have been able to bring herself to speak of her story, or worse, may have been silenced by women unwilling to show compassion.

I am continually amazed at the strength of women who endure horrific challenges. Valiantly, they choose to continue on. Most women who experience this type of pain can testify that the sting of unexpected death never goes away; we just learn to live with it and recognize we are never truly alone. Sometimes women testify in public and private settings of the tangible presence of the Lord during the first few days of trauma, and how they could draw upon His strength when they felt they had none. My good friend Sarah once shared with me, "The Lord comes all the way to the bottom of our pain. There is no depth He cannot reach." To the women who have painfully endured some of life's most difficult hardships, like the woman at the well, we can have faith that the reach and capacity of God knows no limits, and in our moments of loneliness and sorrow, His empathy and presence can heal and lift.

One final story about marriages might be helpful. What if the woman at the well had to leave a husband because *he* was unbearable, or worse, because she felt *she* was unbearable? Has anyone felt the silent hollow of a barren relationship? I recall another friend of mine who married a young man she was introduced to by good friends at a church function. After a covenant marriage, my sweet friend struggled immensely with her new husband. He never seemed to have any space in his life for her, and a great void occupied her heart. It is a sad reality that sometimes a selected spouse behaves one way before marriage and another way after marriage, causing immense heartache, shame, disappointment, and sorrow. Sometime later, she found solace in the arms of another man who had the initial capacity to offer comfort, acceptance, and love. Heartbroken but optimistic, she shared with me she was leaving her first husband to try again with a second man. Unfortunately, after several years her second relationship failed too. Sadly, she journeyed through the long process of a second divorce and hastily entered into a third relationship. Only a few years later, embarrassed and humiliated, my friend was signing divorce papers again. Reaching out one day, she asked, "Will I ever be happy? I've never really been loved. I don't know what love is. Maybe marriage is not for me." It is possible that the woman at the well had the beginnings of one faithful marriage, only for it to turn out poorly, and all subsequent marriages just fell into shambles. Can you imagine the effect this may have had on her self-worth and the weight of negative social stigmas placed on her? Do you see the need in her life to be visited by the Lord? It seems only He could lift her from the depths of embarrassment, loneliness, and rejection.

Devotion and Shackles

My favorite character trait I see in the woman at the well is what I believe to be her religious education and devotion. After the no doubt awkward conversation about her past, she changed the subject and initiated a dialogue about her knowledge of religious heritage and the damming of cultural boundaries. She recalls:

> Our fathers worshipped in this mountain; and ye say, that in Jerusalem is the place where men ought to worship.
>
> Jesus saith unto her, Woman, believe me, the hour cometh, when ye shall neither in this mountain, nor yet at Jerusalem, worship the Father.
>
> Ye worship ye know not what: we know what we worship: for salvation is of the Jews. But the hour cometh, and now is, when the true worshippers shall worship the Father in spirit and in truth: for the Father seeketh such to worship him.
>
> God is a Spirit: and they that worship him must worship him in spirit and in truth. (John 4:20–24)

In the text, I see her intellectual ability to contend with and engage in a theological discussion with a Jewish man. She knew the generational history of worshippers on their holy mountain, which included the line of her matriarchal mothers—Sarah, Rebekah, Leah, and Rachel—and how access to the venue of worship, the Jerusalem temple, was eventually denied to the people of Samaria and designated solely for the Jews. She had a desire to worship in the temple, but because she was a woman of Samaria, she could not.

Sometimes God comes to us to release us from barriers that prevent us from realizing our fullest potential. Barriers can include cultural traditions, doctrinal confusion, doubts, self-doubt, and sin. One of the most beautiful aspects of this story is the fact that Jesus validated her claim and acknowledged the current cultural boundary that to obtain salvation one must worship in the way of the Jews, which denied her personal access to the temple, and ultimately to God. Then, like only God can, He sought to release her from her shackles and taught that she would one day soon worship not at a specific location per se, but essentially wherever she is, so long as her worship was built upon *spirit and truth*. Imagine the feeling she must have had when she learned the possibility that religious shackles and cultural boundaries might soon be broken. This meant she could worship! If she truly felt shackled by doubts and cultural barriers that blocked her ability to worship, it seems she clung to the prophecy of a promised Messiah.

Perhaps full of questions, emotions, and even conviction, she offered her final statement regarding religious devotion: "I know that Messias cometh, which is called Christ: when he is come, he will tell us all things" (John 4:25). Only He could accomplish the monumental task of breaking cultural barriers and opening opportunities for worship to all.

Let me illustrate how we too can overcome religious shackles in a story about one of my favorite friends, Paige, who has since married my brother. When Paige was in her teenage years, she expressed to me her desire to worship God more fully, yet like the woman at the well, internal struggles and doubts plagued her mind. Additionally, an entanglement with a young man at school presented some challenges that were difficult for Paige to navigate on her own, leaving her down-trodden, lonely, and discouraged. Paige attended my seminary class during her junior and senior years of high school. During those seminary years, she wanted to know how and where to worship God, but God seemed a spiritual universe away. In her prayers, she pleaded to know if God loved her and if she would ever have the strength to overcome her struggles and the darkness of doubt.

A couple of years later, Paige had an experience that filled her soul with great joy and peace. One night, Paige dreamed that she was in our seminary classroom and she felt drawn to the hallway door after feeling a familiar presence in the building. In her dream, Paige looked out the door and saw the Savior walking the halls of the church building. There were several early-morning seminary classrooms in our building, and He walked to each class and observed the setting for a moment. Eventually, He stepped inside our classroom, once again observed the seminary class, and then looked at Paige. She carefully focused on His face and met His eyes. Her open heart and spiritual hunger drew Him to her, and her to Him. His beautiful, perfectly bright presence and calming nature impressed upon her soul that He is the Christ, she is known to Him, and that her faith need not lack. In a powerful moment of healing, Paige was released from the shackles of her doubts and completely enveloped by His love for her. Testimony, joy, and light filled her soul to the brim! In the same moment, through His piercing critique, she learned not to take counsel from her doubts and instead to rely on His strength from which she could draw to navigate and persevere the difficult road she traveled.

Just like Paige, Jesus came to release the woman at the well from binding shackles that prevented her from what she felt was true worship. Just like He did with Paige, God seemed a universe away for the lone woman at the well. Jesus implored her to believe that the hour was soon to come that she would worship the Father without regard to her position and status in life, whether she was in Jerusalem, Samaria, or anywhere. Jesus explained to the woman that soon it would be neither in their holy mountain nor the temple in Jerusalem where people would worship the Father. He clarified that the Father was seeking worshippers who would come to Him in spirit and truth, that it would not be solely about law and location.

Just the Right Person

What follows is probably my most favorite line in all scripture. At the pinnacle of their exchange, after she shared with Jesus her desired devotion and religious knowledge, Jesus revealed and testified to *her* His divine identity: "I that speak unto thee am *he*" (John 4:26). Those words, *I that speak unto thee am he,* always leap off the page and into my heart. Jesus hand-selected this woman, a woman traditionally *not* beloved by all, *not* praised by all, and *not* without a questionable past to hear His first public announcement of His divine identity. In like manner, the first person to learn of Jesus' ascension into the world was a woman. The first time the mortal Messiah publicly declared His identity was to a woman. And, the first person to see the resurrected Christ, that first Easter morning, was a woman. Ladies, these firsts tell us something special about our worth to God. He not only comes to us, but He also confides in us and selects us to sit in the front rows of heavenly experience!

We are told the woman left her water pot and ran to tell others in the city. In response, the author of John records:

> Many Samaritans from that city believed in him because of the woman's testimony, "Come, see a man, which told me all things that

ever I did: is not this the Christ?" So, when the Samaritans came to him, they asked him to stay with them; and he stayed there two days. And many more believed because of his word. They said to the woman, "It is no longer because of your words that we believe, for we have heard for ourselves, and we know that this is indeed the Savior of the world. (John 4:39–42, RSV)[39]

If she truly had been a woman of ill repute, as interpreted by modern commentators, it seems unlikely anyone would have believed her. Who in the city, most especially the men, would have listened to and appreciated her testimony? Yet, she alone paved the way for Jesus to teach other open-hearted Samaritans. Jesus' disciples had gone into the same town to buy food, and although it seems it was not their purpose to pave the way for the Savior to teach, I wonder if the people of Samaria would have believed the disciples if they, mostly Jews, came proselytizing into their town. Jesus needed someone from the inside to pave the way, someone whom they knew, and someone whose testimony and words they could trust. That person was the lone woman at the well!

Embedded in the narrative we find a woman with religious knowledge, the courage to recognize Jesus was more than a Jew and certainly not her enemy, a humility to endure chastisement, and a personal conviction that there would be a Messiah. After successfully understanding and believing His revealed identity and mission, she promptly left her water pot and went back to the city; not her house, not to the early-morning women, but to men who also sought the Savior of the world. In essence, at least on this day, this woman served as a forerunner for the believing Samaritans who came out of the city to meet Jesus. Upon the sight of their coming, Jesus enthusiastically declared to His disciples who returned from the Samaritan city with purchased food, of which he would not eat, "I have food to eat of which you do not know . . . my food is to do the will of him who sent me, and to accomplish his work . . . I tell you, lift up your eyes and see how the fields are already white for harvest" (John 4:31–38). In sum, according to this narrative, Jesus came to a woman of Samaria who became no less than a missionary companion to the Messiah.

I think there is little doubt that she contributed to the work of the Lord that day. She paved the way for others to come unto Him, to recognize Him as the Christ. It is impossible to know all the details of her life, however. Regardless of speculative interpretation, it seems to me the woman at the well waded through difficult heartache, possible rejection, and a loss of confidence in both man and God. Personally, I like the representation of the opposite poles in this story and marvel at the literary juxtaposition between her lowliness and the holiness of Jesus. Against this backdrop came the Savior of the world and revealed instead the potential of her beautiful soul, complete with character flaws, difficult challenges to navigate, and personal religious devotion. No doubt she thought like Mary, Jesus' mother, who said, "For he hath regarded the low estate of his handmaiden . . . for he that is mighty hath done to me great things; and holy is his name" (Luke 1:48-49). Can you imagine how she treasured that experience?

I believe that God wants us to know we are known by Him, accepted by Him, and visited by Him. He reveals Himself to women, in His time and in His way. To close this chapter, I want to revisit the story about my sweet friend Nancy, who I mentioned earlier. In her wait for God to bless her with a baby, she endured, like the woman at the well, the lowliest of lows and the reality of depression, rejection, and discouragement. Very few in Nancy's life could perfectly empathize with the true depth of her challenges. With consistent hope, she clung to and treasured the image of that little girl from 2003, believing it was from the Lord. And then it happened. In 2015, after nineteen years of the "bitterness of soul," and through the latest technology, Nancy finally had a birth story of her own. Today, a little girl with bright eyes and soft blonde curls framing her face runs into her arms and fills her soul with joy. Nancy testifies, "God revealed His power and came to me. He rescued my soul. It was truly a miracle."

His gifts of goodness, mercy, and truth are beautifully offered to all women. He offers the "water that springs up into *everlasting life*" (John 4:14; emphasis added). As He counseled the woman at the well, "The hour cometh, and now is," for us to "worship the Father in spirit and in truth" (John 4:23). While worshipping, let us patiently bear our burdens, including the ones outside our control, and never lose confidence that Jesus is the Christ, and that He manifests His divine identity, to all of us. Remember, a long time ago, at a well near Samaria, in the *sixth hour*, He came to meet . . . her.

A Sacred Partnership

by Heather Farrell

*And whoso shall receive one such little child in
my name, receiveth me.*

—MARK 9:37

*M*any of the stories we have about women in the scriptures, especially those in which they received divine communication, are annunciation experiences, times when God or an angel announced to them that
they were pregnant or would soon become pregnant. Women like Mary
the mother of Jesus, Hagar, Sarah, Rebekah, Hannah, Samson's mother,
and the Shunammite woman in 1 Kings all had spiritual experiences
before they gave birth to their children.

I have spent years studying the spiritually of birth and listening to
women's stories about their spiritual experiences before, during, and after
giving birth to their children. I can witness that God still gives annunciation experiences to women. There are stories of women who, like Sarah
and Rebekah in the Old Testament, struggled to get pregnant and who,
like those ancient matriarchs, conceived miraculously. Many women have
shared with me how they, like Mary and Elizabeth of the New Testament,
have known the names, gender, and even the missions of their children
before they were born, having been given the information in the temple,
in a dream, or in another type of divine communication.

Other women have received revelation during pregnancy about how
to care for their bodies and their unborn babies, being inspired about
what care provider to see, where to give birth, and what procedures
were right, or not right, for them and their baby. In addition, for many
women the experience of labor and birth is a sacred one, where the veil

between heaven and earth is thin. During labor, a woman is a wide open portal between heaven and earth, bringing another person across the veil into mortal life. I know that for me, many of my most sacred experiences—the times when I have felt God and angels nearest—have been as I have labored, walking through the valley of death, to bring my babies into the light.

President Spencer W. Kimball stated, "Mothers have a sacred role. They are partners with God, as well as with their own husbands, first in giving birth to the Lord's spirit children and then in rearing those children so they will serve the Lord and keep his commandments."[40] If, in her motherhood, a woman becomes a partner with God, then it makes sense that God would speak to her, and even visit her, to discuss their shared partnership over the creation of mortal life. So it is no surprise that we have many stories, ancient and modern, that document the ways in which God has spoken to women giving them revelation and direction concerning their bodies, their babies, and their posterity.

Speaking with the Lord

The story of Rebekah in the Old Testament shows one way in which women have received divine revelation about their unborn children. We read in Genesis 25:21 that after nearly twenty years of marriage, Issac "entreated the Lord for his wife, because she was barren." In response to this prayer the Lord was "intreated of him, and Rebekah his wife conceived." Rebekah's pregnancy was incredibly difficult. Genesis 25:22 tells us that the "children struggled within her," and apocryphal sources tell us that she was in great pain that none of the other women could understand or relieve.[41] Realizing that no one else could help her, Rebekeah went to the Lord, asking Him, "Why am I thus?"

In response to her question, Rebekah heard the voice of the Lord telling her that she was pregnant with twins. Moreover, she carried two nations within her womb, one of which would be stronger than the other. Not only did this explain the pain and struggle that she was feeling within her, but the Lord also gave her information about the future of her children, telling her that (against cultural expectations) the older brother would serve the younger brother. Later we see that this information, given to her by God when her sons were still in her womb, is what prompts Rebekah to secure Issac's birthright blessing for her younger son, Jacob, instead of her older son, Esau (see Genesis 27).

Just like he did for Rebekah, God will speak to us about our divine stewardships over our families—and not just our immediate families but our eternal ones. Rebekah's decision to give Jacob the birthright (which included the priesthood and its ordinances) had far-reaching consequences: it affected her grandchildren, great-grandchildren and, in fact, all the children of the earth, securing for them the promises of the Abrahamic covenant. Though our minds are often most concerned with the here and now, God sees the big picture and sees how our families and our actions will affect future generations. If we go to Him, asking with sincere hearts, He will speak to us and give us revelation that will shape not just *our* future and the future of our children, but the future of many generations yet to come.

Jen, my co-author of this book, shared with me how before the birth of her last child, the Lord spoke to her clearly, just as if He had called her up on the phone to get her attention and spoke to her like a friend talking to a friend. She wrote:

> In the middle of the night, I felt a pull to talk with the Lord in prayer before returning to bed after nursing our newborn daughter. As I knelt at my bedside, the conversation was vivid and I could tell I was in the presence of someone. I heard the Lord tell me, "Jen, you have a son waiting. You need to have another baby." I burst into quiet tears.
>
> "Father, how can I do this? Another baby? Can my body handle it? What will my husband say? He is ready to be done." Then, in a calm and peaceful tone, I clearly heard, "Jen, do not worry, he will be just fine with this commandment. But, you need to hurry . . ." I felt like I could ask the Lord any question, no matter how small, and he would answer it. So I asked, "What about our vehicle situation? My husband is out of work and a student. How can we afford a larger vehicle? In a jovial tone the Lord comforted my fears and gave me peace. I could literally feel Him chuckling at my silly concern regarding a vehicle. I also smiled, despite my tears, and heard, "Jen, do you not know who I am?"
>
> I quietly cried for a moment longer and then asked what was the most important question of our discussion that night. "Okay, Father . . . when?" His answer was very strong. There was not an ounce of my soul that did not understand His response. "Now, Jen. You need to hurry. Your son is waiting to come to your family, but you must hurry." I spent a few more moments in tears, and then I mustered my courage and responded, "Yes, Lord, I will."

I was pregnant the next month and we obtained a different vehicle shortly thereafter. The pregnancy was difficult. However, eight months later, I delivered a healthy baby boy we named Jacob. Two months after he was born, I unexpectedly had to undergo my fourth non-pregnancy related uterine surgery in seven years. My doctor informed me that he would not be able to do this surgery again and that my life would be in danger if I had another baby. Together with my doctor, we made the decision to prevent me from getting pregnant again. A few years later, I had to have a hysterectomy.

If I had followed through with *my* plan, we never would have had our son, since I did not want to have another baby. Even if I had come to the conclusion to have another baby on my own, it is very likely that it would have been too late. Unbeknownst to me, my seven-year window of child-bearing years was closing very quickly. Thankfully God came to me that night to give me an urgent commandment regarding my family.

Like Rebekah's mother, Jen received divine communication concerning her stewardship over her body, her children, and her future family. The Lord spoke to *her,* and it was her job to communicate His message to her husband. The Lord knew the challenges that were ahead for Jen and, just like He did for Rebekah, God worked in partnership with her to help her fulfill her son's divine mission.

Partnering with the Lord

It is important to remember that it is not just pregnant women and mothers to whom God speaks about their eternal families, but all women. It doesn't matter if you are unmarried or unable to have children; God will still speak to you and give you direction about your future and your family. I believe that we can make personal promises and covenants with Him that allow us to pull down power from heaven and help us see more clearly what God's plan for us is. Every woman can be a partner with God in the creation of her family, whether or not she ever bears children.

I love the story of Hannah in the Old Testament because it demonstrates a beautiful partnership between God and a woman. In 1 Samuel we read how Hannah's inability to bear children was a source of deep and painful sorrow for her, made worse on the family's annual trip to the tabernacle. On these trips she was acutely aware of her barren situation and her inability to do anything to change it. Year after year she hoped and prayed for a child, to no avail. Until one year she went to the tabernacle and, in "bitterness of soul" (verse 10) she "vowed a vow" (verse 11) to

God saying, "Oh Lord of hosts, if thou wilt indeed look on the affliction of thine handmaid, and remember me, and not forget thy handmaid, but wilt give unto thine handmaid a man child, then will I give him unto the Lord all the days of his life, and there shall be no razor come upon his head" (1 Samuel 1:11).

The vow that Hannah made was a personal one, a promise between her and God. Like many women, the deepest desire of her heart was to be a mother—to work in partnership with God to bring children to the earth. She had done everything she knew how to accomplish this desire, but she needed His help. She approached Him with a promise, a promise that she would consecrate everything she had to God—even the precious son she might bear—if only He would help her see how she was to become a mother.

This was a powerful promise, one that God heard and honored. Eventually, Hannah did bear a child, a son named Samuel, a name which in Hebrew means "God has heard." God had heard Hannah's vow, had honored Hannah's vow, and had worked in partnership with her to bring her son to earth. In return, Hannah honored her side of their deal. When he was old enough, she took her son to the temple to live and be taught by the high priest Eli. Samuel would later become a great prophet and leader in Israel, a man consecrated to the Lord even before he was born.

My friend Erika shared with me a beautiful story about how, like Hannah, she made a personal covenant with God and how He fulfilled His promises to her. She wrote:

> One day over lunch, I casually told my fiancé that I wanted ten children someday. Neither of us really knew what that entailed, coming from small and medium-sized families ourselves, so we both just laughed and dreamed and imagined ourselves with a big van full of rowdy kids and Cheerios ground into the carpet.
>
> That dream was short-lived, however. About a year after we were married I became pregnant, but the pregnancy ended in an early miscarriage. I was deeply sad, of course, but I learned that miscarriage was actually quite common and that I shouldn't worry for the future. I took comfort from priesthood blessings, and my own patriarchal blessing, which spoke about me as a Mother in Zion. I became pregnant again easily, this time with twins. My joy was only matched by my devastation when I lost them in a late miscarriage. By the time I lost my third pregnancy to miscarriage, I understood that something was profoundly wrong.

I underwent batteries of tests, painful procedures, and humiliating appointments. When none of them turned up a concrete diagnosis, I was told that recurring miscarriage was a mysterious area of medicine with few answers for women like me. I was told that I should just "keep trying."

And so I did, year after agonizing year. Through loss after loss, through sorrow-filled Mother's Day Sundays, through friends' baby showers and birth announcements, through ever-deepening spiritual pain. Infertility affected every part of my life, from my intimate moments with my husband, to my relationship with my body, to my very sense of self. Who was I? What was I doing wrong? What was my purpose? And most urgently, how long was I expected to "keep trying?" At what point would enough be enough?

After my eighth miscarriage, during our eighth year of marriage, I was on the brink of total collapse. I went through a period of profound grief, mourning, and deep soul-searching. I cast my mind back over time, and realized that that casual conversation I'd had with my fiancé so many years before had become a consecrated one, and I entered a personal covenant with the Lord. Over many months of pleading prayers, the Lord and I came to an understanding. I told Him that in my innocence and my ignorance, I had been willing to have ten children—and so I would. I would press on and "keep trying" until I reached ten, and then I would be released, my part of the covenant fulfilled.

Within months, and completely unexpectedly, a little three year-old girl found her way into our home and into our hearts, and by the end of the year we had adopted her and she was sealed to us for time and all eternity. My joy was full.

Within another year, I was pregnant again. This would be my ninth pregnancy, but my tenth baby due to my twin pregnancy. I had no expectation that I would carry this baby to term, but as the pregnancy progressed, my prayers became bolder and bolder. I prayed, as I had so many times before, that I could know whether it was a boy or a girl, and that I could know its name. My prayers were answered, and I knew that she would be a girl, and I knew what she would be named. I prayed that I could feel her move, and I did, at first the flutter of a butterfly, but growing in strength day by day. There were numerous complications, however, and every single day was fraught with worry. I prayed that even if I lost her, that I would be far enough along that I would be able to see her face and hold her in my arms. Against all odds, she held on. And finally, in a burst of wild hope, I prayed that she would be born alive. That, I told the Lord, would be enough.

And so she was, barely. In distress and dangerously small, she was born alive. I heard her cry, saw her face, and held her in my arms. And I still do. In fact, now my arms are completely full—with two beautiful girls—busy, boisterous, and trailing ground Cheerios behind them.[42]

Just like Hannah, my friend Erika made a personal covenant with God, a promise that she would consecrate herself to Him and His will, no matter how difficult it was. God honored her covenant and not only helped her through many difficult times but helped her realize the deepest desire of her heart. I know that God works with all women, no matter what our situation is, to help us fulfill the measure of our creation and assist Him in His great work.

Work and Glory

A few months after my first child was born I attended a BYU football game at Lavell Edwards Stadium. The stadium holds nearly 64,000 people, and that day it was filled to the brim. I sat in my seat and stared in amazement at all the people. I was overcome with the realization that each and every one of them, just like the tiny baby I was holding in my arms, had once been nurtured inside the body of a woman; that for each and every person in that stadium, a woman had labored and shed her blood to give them mortal life. I knew that what I was seeing in the stadium that day, though it felt enormous, was nothing. Billions of people lived, and had lived, on earth. Billions of women, all throughout history, had created, carried, nurtured, suffered, and even given their lives to bring forth human life. It filled me with awe.

Then, like a lightning bolt it hit me that for each of those people, all of those billions of people, Christ too had suffered and bled. In that moment, sitting high in the bleachers (paying no attention to the football game) I saw so clearly the masterpiece that is human life, mortal and immortal, and the great role that women have to play in its creation.

In Moses 1:39 God tells us that His work and His glory "is to bring to pass the immortality and eternal life of man." It is important to remember that immortal and eternal life are not possible until we first have *mortal* life, which is given to us by our mothers. Women, through their willingness to bear and nurture children, help make God's great plan of happiness possible. In the great work of bringing forth life and directing it toward the light, God is woman's partner; she brings forth mortal life and He transforms that life into eternal life.

This partnership can be seen beautifully in the New Testament when, after Jesus' death, Mary Magdalene and the other women came to prepare His body properly for death. We might wonder, why? Why were these women worried about Christ's body? In the great haste to have it buried before the Sabbath began, it had been prepared and wrapped by Joseph of Arimathea and others without the ointments and customary care that normally would be given a body. Yet, it was buried. A great stone had been rolled in front of the tomb to seal the body in, and it had lain dead for three days. So why bother?

Pearl S. Buck answered this question beautifully when she wrote about her mother, Carrie, who lost three children to sickness during her time as a missionary in China in the 1880s. Buck wrote: "Once I heard someone say of another's dead child, 'The body is nothing now, when the soul is gone.' But Carrie simply said, 'Is the body nothing? I loved my children's bodies. I could never bear to see them laid into the earth. I made their bodies and cared for them and washed them and clothed them and tended them. They were precious bodies.'"[43]

To these women, who for so long had taken care of Jesus' body, who had fed Him, clothed Him, and seen to His physical needs, His body was precious. Even in death, when His spirit no longer inhabited His body, they were still caring for it. So it is beautiful that while they were on this errand, attending to His body, Christ appeared to them as a gloriously resurrected being. He demonstrated to them His victory over death. Never again would a body lay forever in the grave; all those precious bodies, bodies created and cared for by women, would live again.

It is also significant to note that there are ten stories in the scriptures about people being raised from the dead, and of these ten miracles six of them were either women who were raised from the dead or loved ones who were raised from the dead on behalf of women.[44] In the New Testament we see that Christ raised three people from the dead. First, after being moved to compassion by her grief, Jesus brought the Widow of Nain's son back from the dead (see Luke 7:11–17). Second, even though it was her father who ran through the streets seeking Jesus' aid for his daughter, Jairus' daughter was raised from the dead in the presence of both her father and her mother; and lastly, Lazarus, over whose death Jesus wept freely, was released from the tomb in the presence of his sisters

Mary and Martha. Christ's demonstration to these women that He had the power to reverse physical death seems to illustrate the beautiful partnership between God and women, in which one brings forth mortal life and the other raises that life to immortality.

Saviors on Mount Zion

The sacrifices that women make to bring forth mortal life parallel those made by the Savior. In the New Testament Jesus explained to Nicodemus that a man must be "born again," and that unless he "be born of water and the spirit, he cannot enter into the kingdom of God" (John 3:3, 5). Nicodemus, confused about how a man could re-enter his mother's womb, failed to see the parallel Jesus was making; that the sacrifice required for immortal life in His father's kingdom was similar to the sacrifice required for mortal life on earth, a sacrifice made by women.

The Lord told Moses, "Inasmuch as ye were born into the world by water, and blood, and the spirit . . . even so ye must be born again into the kingdom of heaven, of water, and of the spirit and be cleansed by blood, even the blood of mine Only Begotten; that ye might be sanctified from all sin, and enjoy . . . eternal life in the world to come, even immortal glory" (Moses 6:59). Often when I partake of the sacrament I think how miraculous it is that, like my mother who literally gave her flesh and her blood to give me life, I am being re-created, born again, by partaking of Jesus' flesh and blood.

This immense sacrifice on the part of women can bring with it a oneness with God that is unique. I remember sitting in a Sunday School class in which the Atonement was being discussed. The man teaching the lesson mentioned that he could not imagine how much love the Savior has that He would suffer great pain and agony on our behalf. I didn't raise my hand, but I wanted to. I wanted to tell him that, though I could in no way comprehend the magnitude of pain and suffering endured by our Savior in the Garden of Gethsemane, I *could* understand that type of love. That in giving birth to my children I had willingly, just like the Savior, shed my blood and gone through excruciating pain and hardship to give them life. I had been to that place, the place in the garden where the agony becomes so great that you cannot bear it on your own. The place where God, like He did for Jesus, sent "an angel from heaven" (Luke 22:43) and strengthened me so that I could do for someone else what they could not do for themselves.

As women we understand the love of the Savior, the type of love that makes you willing to give your own life—if necessary—for someone else. A young mother wrote,

> How is it that a human being can love a child so deeply that you willingly give up a major portion of your freedom for it? How can mortal love be so strong that you voluntarily subject yourself to responsibility, vulnerability, anxiety, and heartache and just keep coming back for more of the same? What kind of mortal love can make you feel, once you have a child, that your life is never, ever your own again? Maternal love *has* to be divine. There is no other explanation for it. What mothers do is an essential element of Christ's work. Knowing that should be enough to tell us the impact of such love will range between unbearable and transcendent, over and over again, until with the safety and salvation of the very last child on earth, we can [then] say with Jesus, "[Father!] I have finished the work which thou gavest me to do."[45]

There really is something divine about maternal love, something that touches the very brink of heaven. As Elder Jeffery R. Holland said, "No love in mortality comes closer to approximating the pure love of Jesus Christ than the selfless love a devoted mother has for her child. . . . In fact, [they] are saviors on Mount Zion."[46] In her motherhood, a woman learns to love like the Savior loves, something that brings the Savior and the power of His Atonement very near.

The Masterpiece of Human Life

In the New Testament, when asked by His disciples who was the greatest in heaven (a conversation they seemed to have often), Jesus took a child in His arms and told them that "whosoever shall receive one of such children in my name, receiveth me: and whosoever shall receive me, receiveth not me, but him that sent me" (Mark 9:37). This scripture is quite remarkable. First, it is incredible to think that when we are willing to bring a child to the earth, when we are willing to receive one of God's precious children into our arms, we are receiving Jesus Christ.

Yet even more than that, each and every child who comes to earth, whether they are born in the richest home in Europe or the poorest slum in Asia, is a child of God, a divine son or daughter made in the image of God. When we receive one of these little ones into our homes, into our arms, and into our lives, we are receiving God.

President Spencer W. Kimball reaffirmed this when told women:

> This is a partnership. God and his creation. The Primary song says, "I am a child of God." Born with a noble birthright. God is your father. He loves you. He and your mother in heaven value you beyond any measure. They gave your eternal intelligence spirit form, just as your earthly mother and father have given you a mortal body. You are unique. One of a kind, made of the eternal intelligence which gives you claim upon eternal life.
>
> No matter what you read or hear, no matter what the differences of circumstances you observe in the lives of women about you, it is important for you Latter-day Saint women to understand that the Lord holds motherhood and mothers sacred and in the highest esteem. He has entrusted to his daughters the great responsibility of bearing and nurturing children.
>
> This is the great, irreplaceable work of women. Life cannot go on if women cease to bear children. Mortal life is a privilege and a necessary step in eternal progression. Mother Eve understood that. You must also understand it.[47]

I had a very special experience when I was pregnant with my first child that gave me a glimpse of how much God values mothers and what divine work it is. It happened during the childbirth class my husband and I were taking. The instructor asked us to breathe deeply and imagine ourselves in a peaceful place. I started envisioning myself on a sandy beach with the ocean lapping at my feet but quickly felt uncomfortable. Then, almost immediately my mind shifted and I found myself sitting in the celestial room of the Bountiful Utah Temple. This was the temple where I received my endowment and has always had special significance in my life.

As I sat there, my soul became infused with peace and joy, and I saw my unborn son. He was a young man, tall, blond, and clothed in white. He approached me and called me "Mother." I felt power in that word and knew that it was a title or respect, the grandest, noblest title he could call me by. I then saw the Savior standing beside him, holding a book. It was the book of my son's life. He handed me the book and opened it to the page where my son's life on earth was to begin. It was a very thick book, and I was amazed to see that He opened the book in the middle. There were many pages that were already written on, hundreds of pages, and I realized that my son's life was not beginning with birth; it was continuing. As I looked into my son's eyes and the eyes of my Savior, I saw in them immense gratitude for my willingness to be my son's mother and guide him in his earthly journey.

My son is now a teenager, and sometimes it is hard to remember that this boy is the same young man I saw in my vision. Yet he is, and when the days get long and the job of mothering seems thankless, I try to remember him as I saw him then. I try to remember that his life did not begin on earth and it will not end here. He is a child of God, created in the image of God, and through the miracle of Christ's Atonement he can become a glorified and eternal being. He is, as Marion G. Romney said, "a god in embryo,"[48] and it is incredible to know that the body I have created for him will never die. It will live on throughout eons of time.

The creation of life, mortal and immortal, is a beautiful partnership between God and women, and one in which God is not a silent partner. He has always, and still does, speak to women and give them divine guidance about their stewardship over the gateway of life. He sees the past, the present, and the future, and all the children yet to come. He can, and will, give you revelation and direction to know how you can assist Him in bringing souls to earth, nurturing them, and guiding them back to God. If your heart is open and willing to listen, He will speak to you, just like He spoke to women of old. He will guide you as you help to bring forth His work and His glory, the immortality and eternal life of all His children. Life is God's masterpiece.

Just between Us

by Jen Mabray

*As each has received a gift, employ it for one
another, as good stewards of God's varied grace.*

−1 PETER 4:10, RSV

*A*t times I am earnestly asked if I believe in angels. To be honest, I love this question! It makes me smile to consider the possibilities of angelic ministrations. Paul speaks of ministering angels in his letter to the Hebrews and says we might not even notice they are involved in our lives (see Hebrews 1:14, 13:2).

Traditionally angels are thought to be just beyond our mortal vision, whose privilege it is to minister to us in the name of God. Sometimes, angels are considered to have power over the elements, like water and fire, and have superhuman strengths to carry out the work of God (see Revelation 7:1, 14:18, 16:3–5, 12). An angel came to the Apostle Peter while in prison the night before he was to be executed, broke the chains that bound him, and bid Peter to follow him outside the walls (Acts 12:1–11). Some angels also bear messages of hope and love, and are sent to teach His word. While examples in scripture typically ascribe angels to be genderless, there is one verse in Zechariah that says "two women" appeared with "wind in their wings" to teach Zechariah about the symbolism of sacred objects in the house of the Lord (Zechariah 5:9).

I believe mortal women play an important role in the angelic ministry of God, and are called upon to lengthen His reach, through various mediums and capacities within our families, our church congregations, at work, at school, on the internet, and on the other end of the phone line. Narrowing the idea even further, I believe God reaches *through* women *to* women through our special capacity to foster deep connections and build relationships upon foundations of love, trust, and innate understanding. This is not to say that God does not reach through men to come to women, for certainly this is true. Thankfully, it is true! An article in *Forbes Magazine* says the edification of women stems from the "Power of the Pack," and proclaims, "There is a special place in heaven for women who support other women."[49] I would add the highest level of feminine empowerment happens in the name of God and through honest collaboration.

Maybe He knows He can reach more and reach faster if women are a conduit to women. For example, "Mom-squads" (moms collaborating together to raise children) provide mothers a safety net of personal experiences to draw much-needed confidence to raise children; teams of women in the workplace create strong professional relationships that provide a springboard of motivation to stay focused, overcome hurdles, and set goals; women in religious organizations connect through spiritual discussion, fellowship and gatherings, mutual trust, and common morals; and women who are more independent in their endeavors sometimes meet with a friend one-on-one for mutual edification and connection.

Women are important for the growth of women. We are teachers, thinkers, artists, musicians, mothers, believers, motivators, leaders, nurturers, healers, scientists, physicians, soldiers, fighters, ministers, missionaries, lovers, athletes, philosophers, and helpers. In essence, by divine design, we are doers. I can't hear your answer, but I'm going to ask anyway. Why do you do the things you do for other women? To inspire? To help, to teach, or to lift? Maybe to connect? I know a fire burns in your bones to do good for others. And God needs doers to reach the lives of others. President Russell M. Nelson, a father of nine daughters, elaborated in a 1989 general conference, "To help [each other] reach [our] celestial potential is part of the divine mission of woman. In partnership with God, her divine mission is to help spirits live and souls be lifted. This is the measure of her creation. It is ennobling, edifying, and exalting."[50]

Mothers and daughters, sisters and grandmothers, empty-nesters and never-nesters, friends and co-workers, bride-tribes and mom-squads, this chapter is a collection of God's reach from woman to woman, and is dedicated to you. The stories are true, and most are written in first person, aside from two stories I selected from the Bible to show the potential relationships of ancient women and God's reach. The two biblical narratives sandwich the modern stories and include a representation and light interpretation of biblical facts. I gave enough of the story to push your own imagination to consider the dialogues between biblical women and the impact of God in their lives.

I hope the stories below warm your heart and touch your soul. Grab a snuggly blanket, a cup of hot cocoa . . . and if you're prone to tears, maybe grab a tissue, too. Each story below illuminates God's reach *through* women *to* women. Remember His power can edify and lift, teach and mold, strengthen and perfect, and it is our privilege to assist Him in this great work. Sometimes, the work is just between us.

Jochebed and Miriam

Miriam and her mother, Jochebed, are two empowered women who help one another during immense challenges at the beginning of the Hebrew Exodus story from Egypt (see Exodus 1–2). Traditionally, when this story is told, we tend to hear only of Moses and his mission to save the Israelites. His mother, Jochebed, and his sister, Miriam, occupy supportive roles. Instead of recalling this story with Moses as the prominent character, I want to place him in the position of a supportive role and focus solely on Miriam and her mother, Jochebed. When I do this, I see how two women embodied the concept of God's reach through woman to woman.

When Jochebed, a Levite, gave birth to her son, she feared greatly for his life. Based on a threat of insurrection and the potential for another Hebrew slave revolt, Pharaoh ordered "all the infant Hebrew sons to be thrown into the Nile" to curb the growing population of the children of Israel (Exodus 1:9–22). Jochebed hid her newborn for three months and then likely in immense sorrow, she did as Pharaoh commanded. In an ark or basket-type vessel, made waterproof by pitch, Jochebed released her precious infant son into the Nile (see Exodus 2:3). I imagine her anguish was unlike anything else she had ever experienced as the little basket floated away from her grasp. If you've never listened to the Israeli singer Ofra Haza sing "Deliver Us" from *The Prince of Egypt,* now would be a good time. She mesmerized score writer Hans Zimmer with her depiction of Jochebed's agonizing defeat through melodic ululation (voice wavering or trill used in the Arab world), and film artists decided to draw Jochebed to look like Ofra.

We are told Miriam watched the precious river-cargo float among the reed flags and eventually into the hands of the daughter of Pharaoh. Personally, I like to think Miriam tended the little ark, keeping it afloat and anchored in the more gentle waters along the bank. Like a shepherdess who guides her flock, Miriam tended her baby brother until he was safe. Biblical scholars are unsure how old Miriam was at this time, but I think it would be safe to assume she was old enough to have already developed a nurturing heart. No doubt it pained her terribly to witness the torment of her mother, and it was difficult to make sense of Pharaoh's paranoia when he ordered the killing of innocent babies. When Miriam accompanied the tiny baby down the river, I wonder if she had a motherly connection to her brother. I am the oldest girl in my family, and in my young-girlhood years, I felt as if each new baby that came to my parents was somehow *my* baby too. Miriam likely had a special affection for her baby brother, and it appears as if she had the faith to consider he would be safe or conversely, the courage to witness the drowning currents of the Nile.

We know the baby landed safely in the arms of a compassionate daughter of Pharaoh. Through quick wit and the capacity to speak out, Miriam offered to the woman, "Shall I go and call to thee a nurse of the Hebrew women, that she may nurse the child for thee?" (Exodus 2:7). No doubt the baby, who would be named Moses by Pharaoh's daughter, began to cry and needed nourishment. With certainty Pharaoh's daughter was pleased to learn another woman, perhaps close by, had the capacity to nurse and comfort him.

Looking at this episode from a woman's perspective, if we ask certain questions, we can create a framework of God's reach through one woman to help another. Try to answer these questions. Who comforted Jochebed when she put her baby into the Nile? Who prompted Miriam to guide the floating ark into the arms of an Egyptian woman? Who gave Miriam the idea to call her mother right back to the child, and to her breast? Who softened the heart of Pharaoh's daughter to refute her father's murderous command, which in turn gave her an opportunity to also be a mother? The answer to every question could easily be God.

Now, if we answer these same questions from a foundation that God reaches through women to women, and ask who the participants were in each miracle, we will see that each woman's desperate plea was answered by another woman. In essence, the women in the story were conduits for God's hand to help someone else. God was able to reach Jochebed through Miriam, who secured a job for her mother as a wetnurse for her biological son, which saved Jochebed from having to witness the murder of her baby. God reached through a daughter of Pharaoh to comfort Miriam, who must have breathed a sigh of relief when the little ark was spotted and the baby was taken into her arms. Pharaoh's daughter clearly desired to raise a child of her own, else she would have killed the baby or given it to another. We later learn through Jochebed's courage to release her son to be raised by an Egyptian princess, God reached the children of Israel by calling Moses to lead them from Egyptain bondage.

It is because of God's reach through each of these women that they were able to reach each other. In the same way today, God still uses our courage, goodness, intellect, obedience, wit, and selfless sacrifice to reach more of His children. Sometimes, our efforts are small and to us seem insignificant. I think, like the still small voice often gives us a feeling or a thought, God's reach can be just as simple. When we allow God to reach through us to another, perhaps only God can see the full measure of the impact. See if you can spot God's reach in the following true-story accounts.

Mekenzie and Her Mother

One Sunday morning, Mekenzie bore a powerful witness that God speaks with His daughters and hears their prayers after a transformative experience she had during family prayer. That particular family prayer began like every other in their home, with Mekenzie and her siblings eagerly awaiting to say amen as they knelt beside their parents in the living room. Her mother always prayed using a "prayer voice," a voice more reverent, contemplative, and resonant with respect toward God. "That night was different though," Mekenzie explained. "Her voice was deeper, softer, sort of angel-like, and full of emotion."

"Dear Heavenly Father . . . " her mother began. Suddenly, Mekenzie noticed the pitch of her mother's voice changed, even from her normal "prayer voice." Without expecting anything, but just curious about the change of inflection, Mekenzie opened her eyes. In her mind's eye, a dreamy-type glow surrounded her mother as she knelt, arms folded, and head reverently bowed in respect to the Almighty. Right there in their living room, Mekenzie felt as if she witnessed her mother *speak to God.*

Mekenzie shared, "My mom had a different voice, quieter, more reverent. She spoke with such emotion and prayed for each of us by name." In that very moment, as Mekenzie heard her name mentioned before the Lord, a spiritual warming filled her soul. Her name was mentioned to God, and she felt as if an unseen blanket enveloped her in His love.

Prayer was common during Mekenzie's teenage years. Today, she leads her own life and still draws from her mother's living example on how to approach God in holy supplication. Mekenzie knows sacred texts teach how to best communicate with God, what words honor Him as our Creator, and how to give praise and thanksgiving for the blessing of His Son, Jesus Christ. Along with her treasured knowledge and understanding of sacred texts, Mekenzie cherishes most her mother's example.

"She taught me how I should speak to God and who He could be to me, simply by the way her inflection changed when she spoke with God." Drawing upon the imagery of that one memorable, yet ordinary evening prayer, Mekenzie gained anchoring faith that God listens to His daughters. She testified of her mother, "I knew without a doubt that her prayers reached heaven."

A Woman in Tucumcari, New Mexico, and Me

Years ago, my husband, kids, and I were driving back to Dallas after a ski trip to Park City, Utah. Our travel plan would take us through New Mexico on the Sunday morning before Christmas, and I thought it would be nice to stop for sacrament meeting. I calculated we would be in Tucumcari, New Mexico, around 9 a.m. and could make a morning service. Just after I clicked off the map on my phone, I had the feeling I needed to call a leader in the Tucumcari ward and ask if they needed a pianist for Christmas.

Directed by the missionaries to the ward music chair, I explained our desire to attend their ward for Sunday services and asked if she needed a pianist for anything. She let out a gasp and cried, "Who told you to call me? How did you know to call me? I was in the middle of a prayer to the Lord, asking for help, and the phone rang!" Still sniffling, she explained they had no musician for their Christmas service and when she asked the bishop what they should do, he promised the Lord would take care of them and they would have a lovely service. I felt like her spirit spilled through the phone and into my heart as she witnessed God's reach. She testified, "He attends to even the finite details of our lives." I was witnessing His reach too, through the phone, and with a woman I had yet to meet.

She quickly interviewed me over the phone to see if I could play what she had selected. "No problem at all," I responded. "Anything else you would like me to play? I play well enough to sight read any hymn and elaborate most pieces to be a special musical number on the spot."

"Can you play the organ?"

"Yes, I sure can."

Our family had a lovely Christmas Sunday service with a tiny ward in Tucumcari, New Mexico. The spirit of Christmas was palatable and pierced our hearts as we sang a wonderful selection of hymns, listened to special numbers, and contemplated carefully crafted talks on the birth of the Savior.

As I looked out over the congregation from the piano and organ benches, I noted my family of six added greatly to their numbers. The bishop asked from the pulpit if we would like to move to their area, for they surely could use us. My kids laughed and shrugged their shoulders, and Todd and I exchanged glances. For us, it was a memorable pass-through sacrament meeting. For the ward, it was special to have a musician and a cute little family join their congregation. For me, my heart was filled to the brim to share my musical ability. For the music chair, she was so tickled that God came to her rescue with an immediate solution to her simple heart-felt plea—a pianist for Christmas Sunday.

Julie and Tresa

"I have to push!" Julie screamed as she clung to the headrest of her car, her body turned around to face the back seat. Her large swollen belly almost reached the seat-back as she knelt. *This is not happening! This is not happening! Oh Father! This is not what we planned for!*

"Julie . . . listen to me." Tresa's voice floated in and out of Julie's mind as she tried to stay focused amidst everything that was going wrong. "You're not going to push, you're going to pant with me! Together okay . . . one, two, in, out."

"We can't go to Lehi. She won't make it. Get to Payson, fast!" Tresa directed to Julie's husband, Chris. With great desire to ease his wife's agony, Chris pushed their little Nissan Sentra to its max and sped through any intersection he could without putting everyone in danger, hoping they would reach the hospital or meet the ambulance en route before the baby came. Tresa was on the line with another woman from 9–1–1 dispatch in the back of the car. The woman ordered Tresa and Chris to pull over. They were so close, but there was no more time. Chris brought the car to a quick halt on the side of the road and jumped out to assist Tresa by working quickly to remove Julie's lower clothing.

"I can't do this! Heavenly Father please help me!" Julie pleaded aloud. "I can't do this!" Alternating between two experienced women, 9-1-1 dispatch gave an order, and Tresa coached. Order. Coach. Order. Coach. Crouched in a blanket of new-fallen snow, on the side of the road, Chris knelt beside the open car door while Tresa coached Julie to deliver her firstborn son in the front seat of a little car. "Are you ready, Julie?" "Okay, honey . . . push!"

When I interviewed Julie, she tenderly disclosed, "Jason's birth was pretty intense. I remember thinking, 'I can't do this, I can't do this.'" An emergency delivery in the front seat of a little car was not how Julie saw herself having a baby, but everything happened so quickly, and she progressed faster than anyone had anticipated. Thankfully, Tresa, Julie's friend and an experienced doula, had the capacity to support Julie through the wave of each contraction and remain calm during the most intense moments of her labor. She also coached Chris on how to "catch" his newborn son. Julie said, "I needed encouragement, peace, direction, and permission to move forward, especially since everyone initially told me, *don't push!*"

After Tresa and the woman from 9-1-1 dispatch discerned the situation and knew it was time for the baby to come, they gave Julie permission to push. She recalled, "I immediately gained peace and confidence to have this baby, and everything unfolded like a revelation." Julie explained, "Although it was super traumatic, it was also extraordinarily spiritual. I reached out to Heavenly Father in prayer, because I really needed His help, and I was immediately answered—Tresa and the woman from 9-1-1 dispatch were right there! They were the answer, *my* answer!"

Sarah and Janet

Sarah sat in my living room and with great conviction, testified, "I believe women need women. We have been endowed with a divinely appointed power to help other women. That power enables us to fill in the gaps and voids created from the challenges of mortality."

Jesus taught about opposition in all things (see 2 Nephi 11, 15). Sarah explained, "Opposition isn't limited to certain areas of our lives. We are here to experience opposition in all things. Inspired by God's love, women often assist other women to fill in the gaps created from opposition. That's what Janet did for me."

Sarah shared that she grew up in a religious home and expressed gratitude that she learned about God. However, at church, her parents would step out of their "home personalities," and as if they were acting in a play, perform their "church personalities." Her parents had praiseworthy "church personalities," but outside of church, Sarah and her siblings had to endure a difficult and harmful home life. "My childhood left me confused about the roles of motherhood, parenting, and my personal value to God. I felt like I was a wandering soul and ultimately, I worried my relationship with God was similar to my relationship with my father . . . that I would never be good enough to deserve his love."

In her late teens, Sarah began to notice that her family situation was not healthy but did not have the ability to articulate her struggles or navigate a pathway to healing. After Sarah served a church mission and married her husband, sadly a toxic residue from her long exposure to harmful parenting began to manifest itself through horrible pains in her gallbladder, an ever-present rash that appeared on her arms, hair loss, and a debilitating fatigue that overcame her ability to think, feel joy, or function with any kind of endurance.

Janet entered Sarah's life, by way of a mutual friend, and learned of Sarah's struggles. She too had encountered immense hardships in her life through which she learned how to rely on Jesus Christ. A few decades older than Sarah, Janet became a loving mother to Sarah, and for the first Sarah felt unconditional love.

During my conversation with Sarah, I felt the power of her endearing admiration for Janet as she joyfully and tearfully shared the impact Janet had in her life. Janet was an agent of the reach of God to Sarah, which brought much-needed healing, knowledge, and self-confidence. At one point, I thought about some of the poetic psalms written by David, and the words of Isaiah, both of whom honored God for offering His strength and guidance in their lives. Considering the concept of honor, I had the idea to ask Sarah to craft a "psalm" for Janet to find as a way to honor her.

Dear Janet,

I want you to know, for the first time in my life, you showed me the unconditional love of a mother. You saw potential in me and helped me to be my best without burning out. You gave me permission and confidence to be myself, to laugh, and to understand that I have value.

Janet, I am filled with tears when I consider how much I needed your care. You filled a mother's role for me, which I had never before experienced. You looked at me and I knew you loved me—just because

I existed! My life has taught me a great deal about opposition and I believe we will have struggles in areas that we do not feel we deserve to be tested. Now, I thank Heavenly Father for opposition, which during my early twenties, led me to your loving arms. Through your God-given strengths, you tenderly reached back and filled the gaping void from my childhood with the healing balm of love and care.

Janet, you taught me to balance service and self-care. You taught me Yoga! Oh, how I loved all those many days when you pushed back your sofa and showed me how to quiet my mind and listen to my body. Your professional knowledge helped me return to health as you narrowed down and eliminated food products from my diet that my body could no longer handle. You showed me how to cook, plant greens, and eat better. Eventually, I could run again without getting winded. Remember that time you encouraged me to cut sugar out completely? It was awesome!

Janet, I noticed immediately your testimony of Christ, your ability to be in tune with the spirit, and your observation of others with your eyes and heart. You helped give me a proper foundation to grow in my testimony of Jesus Christ. I believe we have Heavenly Parents, even a Heavenly Father and a Heavenly Mother, both equally endowed with power, glory, wisdom, and love! When I consider *Her* image, I think of you.

Janet, like only a mother can do, you taught me the positive influence of motherhood, womanhood, self-esteem, and healthy boundaries. You encouraged me to surround myself with others who could help and to be resilience in difficult situations. Your wisdom prepared me for future events, like when I moved 5000 miles away to Russia to teach elementary school. When I became a mother, I decided to strive to be the kind of mother you exemplified to me.

Thank you, Janet, for doing for me what I desperately needed. Thank you for loving me, caring for me, and teaching me. Thank you, Janet, for being a . . . *mother.*

Always your daughter,
Sarah

Julie and Kristi

In early 2020, Julie hoped someone could stay with her through the next twenty-four hours. The next day was the fourth anniversary of her dad's suicide.

Grief is overwhelming, no matter the cause of death. Suicide grief is particularly complicated and messy. For survivors, the calendar marches forward, and suddenly you find yourself coming upon that dreadful month and then *that* day again. Anticipation leading up to the day involves constant and relentless playbacks of the trauma. In addition, survivors are forced to confront the negative stigma associated with that kind of loss. Unfortunately, this silences the survivor while they work through many years of despair and suffocating depression, often alone.

Julie was used to the associated wounds from suicide loss, but the thought of coming upon another anniversary was overwhelming. She wondered if anyone noticed the intensity of her pain, especially since it had now been four years. Without knowing Julie's lonesome struggles, her Relief Society president, Kristi, was browsing Facebook earlier that day and found that Julie would soon have a difficult anniversary to manage. Working quickly on heaven's errand, she purchased some flowers, crafted a loving note, and knocked on Julie's front door.

"I know what day it is," she said, a tender expression in her voice. "And, I just want you to know I'm here. I'm not going anywhere."

Tears streamed down Julie's face, and sobs shook her full frame as she stood in the doorway staring at Kristi. *How did you know? Lord, how did she know? Oh Father . . . You came to me. You came to me. Thank you, Lord. Thank you.* With momentary healing in her presence and care, Kristi was the conduit of God's reach to Julie.

Lisa and Wendy

Wendy was kidnapped at the age of twelve and forced into slave-type labor for another family in a foreign country, during which time her loving mother passed away in Honduras. Although not very interested in her life, Wendy's abusive father finally rescued her, passed her to other families, and occasionally took her into his household. Unfortunately, he lived with several other men, and Wendy was again subjected to a dangerous and hellish situation.

In an attempt to save Wendy, a life-saving teacher asked the father if Wendy could live with her and her husband. Wendy quickly fell in love with her "foster" family, but due to serious medical complications in the household, Wendy needed to move again. In a heart-wrenching phone call to a friend named Lisa, Wendy's foster mother asked if it was possible for the now seventeen-year-old girl to move in with Lisa's family.

Lisa's mind swirled with concerns. *How does this work with my teenage son? What about my other four children? I only speak English, and Wendy is still very dependent on Spanish. How will we communicate? What about legal documents . . . if she gets sick . . . and what about her schooling?* That night Lisa poured her heart to God, laid her concerns at His feet, and received a priesthood blessing. Tremendous peace and an overwhelming thought pierced her soul: *Wendy is My daughter . . . fear not to do good.* With great confidence, Lisa responded in the return phone call, "We can take her."

Four distinct miracles happened during Wendy's stay with Lisa's household. Each miracle testified to Lisa that Wendy was indeed His daughter, and He had a plan to reach her through the righteous intentions and obedience of willing women.

Miracle 1: Shortly after Wendy arrived at Lisa's home, she became terribly sick and needed to go to the hospital, but without legal authority, Lisa feared no hospital would accept her. Permission was needed from Wendy's legal guardian, her abusive and often drunk father, who had previously denied permission for Wendy's medical care. The idea was dangerous, and Lisa felt she was toying around with a hornet's nest. Notifying the father would add additional complications to an already complicated scenario. Miraculously, a sober man answered the phone, said yes to treatment, and then hung up without demanding to know where Wendy was or giving any indication that he was coming after her.

Miracle 2: Medical attention at the hospital was the tip of the iceberg, and Wendy continued to suffer without additional treatment. Offering to help, a ministry clinic administered to Wendy without questioning her case file. During that time, the foster agency informed Lisa that because Wendy was seventeen, she could sign for medical treatment herself.

Miracle 3: Women in Lisa's church circle learned of the delicate situation and rallied around Wendy with additional support and love, without judgment or criticism. At Christmas time, one woman felt inspired to make Wendy her own "Angel Tree" ministry recipient. Through her generosity, Wendy received specific gifts that she felt certain no one knew she desired.

Miracle 4: Wendy continued to attend school while she lived with Lisa, whose house was situated outside Wendy's high-school boundaries. In a seamless transition, a woman in the school administration told Lisa, "We will reroute a bus just to pick her up. Don't worry about the logistics. As long as you're honest with us and keep her safe and healthy, we want her to be a kid."

During Wendy's stay, Lisa felt a veil of protection surrounding their family. Wendy witnessed a safe home where young women are loved, valued, educated, and recipients of priesthood blessings. Lisa said, "God speaks very directly when we are about His business. Sometimes, He asks us to navigate uncharted waters, and if we are willing to listen, He will reach through us to guide the life of another." She shared a scripture that she felt guided all her actions: "Fear not to do good, [little family], for whatsoever ye sow, that shall ye also reap; therefore, if ye sow good ye shall also reap good for your reward. . . . Let earth and hell combine against you, for if ye are built upon my rock, they cannot prevail. . . . Perform with soberness the work which I have commanded you. Look unto me in every thought; doubt not, fear not" (selections from D&C 6:33–36).

It was not man's law but God's law that Wendy be cared for. Through the efforts of righteous women willing to step into uncharted waters, God beautifully reached Wendy.

Jenna and Alison

Alison and Jenna will never forget the reach of God that healed Alison's heart through Jenna's selfless sacrifice. On February 9, Alison stood beside her surrogate, Jenna, who gave birth to a healthy full-term baby boy. Alison and her husband, Justin, were about to hold the baby that Alison's body would not allow her to carry and birth for herself. Alison exclaimed about the birth of her son, "It was so amazing and took things to a whole new appreciation for me. I am just speechless someone would do that for us!" A few days after the delivery, when the baby was allowed to go home, Jenna returned to the hospital to see Alison and Justin one more time. In tears and locked in a hug, Alison cried, "I'm still in shock! Thank you so much!! I just love you!" Before Jenna left, she witnessed Alison snuggling her newborn son and thought, *It was only a little time out of my life to give her a lifetime with a child.*

When I interviewed Jenna and Alison, Jenna was near the end of her third trimester with Alison and Justin's baby. Two separate worlds, nearly three hundred miles apart, anxiously awaited the arrival of this very special little boy. Their stories below, told separately and in their words, encompass the reach of God through woman to woman. I believe God knows that sometimes only a woman can reach another woman.

81

Jenna's Side

"I follow a lady on social media who struggled mightily with infertility and miscarriages. When she did finally have a pregnancy that took, in her second trimester, the doctors found that her torso did not allow for the proper growth of her baby's lungs. She held her baby for two weeks, and then he passed away.

"As I tried to imagine her burden, my heart burned and I passionately yearned to help. I thought, *how could I even empathize? My husband and I get pregnant so easily, and I carry so easily—there's really no struggle!* I was pregnant with my fourth baby at the time, and as he eventually transitioned from my womb into my arms. I had an idea of what I could do. . . .

"I prayed about my idea for a long time. I felt like God not only answered me, He motivated me and showed me how I could change lives. Then I heard President Dallin H. Oaks encourage us to take advantage of modern medicine and technology. I had my motivation, my vision, and my confirmation, and I was not going to look back. My husband was shocked when I said I wanted to have another baby, but not a baby for us . . . *I wanted to have a baby for someone else.* I decided to be a surrogate.

"After my first inquiry at a surrogate agency, I was even more excited. I chose to be a gestational surrogate, which means I am solely an incubator for the embryo of another couple. It's all their DNA. Once I listed my parameters, I was placed in something like a dating app where surrogate-seeking couples browsed my bio. I was told my parameters were pretty tight, so it would be a while before the agency found a match. To my surprise, my bio was matched after one month, and my husband and I were invited to a conference call to meet Alison and Justin, who lived in Houston. I prayed, *please Lord, help me to feel either really good, or really bad—nothing in-between.*

"The conference call was AMAZING! Everything felt so right and the spirit was so strong! Two couples from two different Christian faiths came together over the desire to bring a child into this life! I cried. My husband cried! Alison and Justin cried! Alison and Justin had been married for ten years and had a seven-year-old biological daughter rather easily, and then experienced six heartbreaking miscarriages including two failed attempts at IVF, several uterine surgeries, and finally Alison was told by doctors that her body would not keep a baby.

"Guided by the agency, our meetings covered needed dialogues like bodily intake during pregnancy, breastfeeding, baby showers, the delivery, bonding, future communication, social media, and connection vs. disconnection. After passing the required psychiatric evaluation from the agency, and a hysteroscopy in January 2020, I traveled to Houston for the transfer on May 27, 2020. On June 22, 2020, I returned to Houston, and Alison and I heard her baby's heartbeat for the first time.

"Alison came to that first conference call reserved, nervous, excited, and really unable to disconnect from the difficulty of her traumatic past. When I was about twenty weeks along with her baby, she began to feel everything was more normal than her last six pregnancies and started to get excited. I didn't think I would gain a best friend, but we have a special bond, something deeper than what I could have created on my own.

"I feel like Heavenly Father blessed me with the ability be a candidate for surrogacy because one: I have no jealousy or envy, just excitement for Alison, and two: during pregnancy my hormones remain steady, I am pleasant with everyone, I don't get sick, and I have never been the type of mom who connects to my babies in the womb. I fall in love with them as I raise them. My husband supports me and has from the beginning. He likes my sassy pregnant personality and of course all the curves. And finally, my kids know this baby is not their sibling; he belongs to Alison and Justin.

"I want my daughters to know that if one of them cannot carry, surrogacy is an option that one sister can do for another. I want to dispel the misconception that women choose surrogacy just to avoid stretch marks or changes to their body. Women become surrogates because of selflessness, because of love. Heavenly Father has blessed my body, mind, and soul to have babies. My family feels complete, but I am not finished. Through me, God can reach and heal the wounds of another woman. I am totally ready and excited to deliver this baby for, and into, Alison's arms."

Alison's Side

"Who does this for women? Truly?

"Sometimes you hear about a miracle for someone else, and the thought just creeps inside your heart and mind and you wonder why you can't get a miracle, too. I trust God . . . that anything is possible, and just kept telling myself, *maybe it's not time for my miracle.*

"Justin and I have been married for ten years and we have a seven-year-old daughter. When she was two years old, we started trying for number two, and at ten weeks, I miscarried. Five more miscarriages followed. It was a roller coaster. I would hear heart beats on a sonogram, and then a haunting silence. With two of the losses, I had to have several surgeries due to complications with a DNC.

"After the fourth miscarriage, we sought IVF. The extraction process went really well, but after the first IVF transfer, I lost the baby. We switched to a different doctor for a second attempt, one year later. In preparation, my new doctor, Dr. Kim, fixed my thyroid issues, and did a surgery to fix the shape of my uterus. The IVF transfer was smooth, but I lost the baby, again. Utterly devastated, I cried to God, *why is this not working?* I asked Dr. Kim, *if I was your wife, what would you tell me to do?* He said, *honestly, if you were my wife, I would tell you to consider surrogacy. I do not feel confident your body can carry a baby.*

"My husband and I were open to adoption and surrogacy and prayed about options for four months. My father was adopted, and I've always had a soft spot for adoption, but I still had six frozen embryos remaining from the IVF extraction. I questioned, *do I just walk away from them?*

"After much prayer and discussion with our agency, Shared Conception, we decided to pursue surrogacy. I did not want to walk away from our embryos. I had two dear friends offer to be a surrogate for me, but they found their health would not allow for it, and I learned through the experiences of other women that I wanted a little more separation.

"I was told it would be a couple of months to find a match for me. Literally, the next week, Jenna's photo and profile were sent to me in an email. I could not write up a better profile! I saw that we had similar values and her reason for wanting to do this resonated with our prayers. My husband felt skeptical at first, however, within minutes of hearing Jenna's story during our joint interview hosted by the agency, we not only felt so comfortable, we felt Jenna was amazing!

"The decision to partner with Jenna was so easy. We can't say enough good things about her, her personality, her husband, and our agency who made every legal and psychiatric evaluation as easy as possible. I mean, Jenna was a complete stranger and in such a short time, I gained confidence she would not run off with my baby! Thankfully, she's great at communication and so willing to involve me. Once I called her for a bump pic, and she stopped what she was doing right then and sent me a photo! Bump pics come now every week! Literally, she is our walking oven, our walking kangaroo! I cannot put into words how thankful and blessed we are for Jenna and her family! She is an angel on earth and I truly feel like this was God's plan to have her in our life.

"It's crazy to think we began with five years of struggles and infertility. That first miscarriage was the worst. Even now I hate ultrasounds. It was awful and is still so difficult to talk about. I had to have a DNC versus letting it pass on its own because the umbilical cord did not attach and they thought I could bleed out. Sitting in the hospital, I was shaking and someone asked if I was cold. I responded, *no, I'm about to throw up everywhere*. I sort of got used to loss after that. *Is that even a thing?* The first IVF gave me hope again, but when I lost it, all hope went down the drain. That was supposed to be the solution, like it was for so many other women. I felt hopeless, helpless, and wondered why despite all the doctors efforts, the problem was not figured out. I am healthy and wondered, *what did I do? What did I ever do?* I was never angry with God, but I needed help to sort my feelings. My husband said, *we are not in control, and you are clearly trying to be. God is trying to tell us something and we need to listen to His plan.*

"Some people thought we were crazy for continuing to try for a baby and said, *you already have one, just be happy*. I wanted to punch those people! Our daughter is our world, but when people said those things, it made me question myself. I pleaded for clarity, guidance, and peace in our decision.

"Everything fell into place with Jenna and felt so right from the beginning. When we selected the strongest of our six remaining embryos, we literally watched it thaw and it began to expand right before our eyes! I sat right next to Jenna during the transfer, and then waited a dreadful two weeks to find out if it "took." I was at work when I received a phone call that Jenna was pregnant! I just stared at the phone. Weeks later, I had to endure an ultrasound. *Oh God*, I pleaded, *please be with me.* Jenna prayed too. She was very positive and confident and I felt I could only live on her confidence, for I had none. You become very guarded with your thinking when you go through so many miscarriages. I couldn't allow myself to get excited or even consider the reality of the outcome just yet. The sonogram began . . . and I heard and saw a heartbeat.

"On my night stand is a book called *Borrowed Courage*. At the beginning of the book there is a section about the heartache and loss of children/miscarriages. Given the title, I am sure it's a very inspiring story, but I had to stop reading it and have not been able to bring myself to read it to the end. At the moment, I love the title, I need the title. It describes my journey and what I feel about Jenna. I haven't just witnessed Jenna's courage, I've borrowed her courage! I'll finish the book one day, but currently, it holds every ultrasound photo and my fertility bracelet our agency gave me as a gift at our transfer.

"I know God is in control and even though my six miscarriages were a terrible thing, we feel so blessed to be healthy and here. The concept of *Borrowed Courage* is always on my heart, and reminds me to never stop trying, for myself, for my husband, for our daughter who is still too young to really understand. She will one day. For now, she knows now that she has a little brother coming soon and is so excited!"

Elizabeth and Mary

> Fear not, Mary: for thou hast found favour with God. And, behold, thou shalt conceive in thy womb, and bring forth a son, and shalt call his name JESUS. He shall be great, and shall be called the Son of the Highest. . . .
>
> And, behold, thy cousin Elisabeth, she hath also conceived a son in her old age: and this is the sixth month with her, who was called barren. For with God nothing shall be impossible.
>
> And Mary said, Behold the handmaid of the Lord; be it unto me according to thy word. (Selections from Luke 1:30–38)

When the angel left after speaking with Mary, we are told she eagerly traveled to Judea to visit her relative Elisabeth (see Luke 1:39). Can you imagine what types of questions, fears, joy, and excitement she pondered on her journey? When Mary arrived, Elisabeth was overjoyed, and being filled with the Holy Ghost she proclaimed, "Blessed art thou among women, and blessed is the fruit of thy womb . . . as soon as the voice of thy salutation sounded in mine ears, the babe leaped in my womb for joy! (Luke 1:41–44, emphasis added). Elisabeth was completely honored that the mother of her Lord came to see *her* (see Luke 1:43).

I have imagined this scene many times and wondered about the depth of their bond. Not only did they carry babies at similar times, but their pregnancies were also both announced by angels and foretold in prophecy. However, more than just pregnancy and joy bonded their hearts. If we take a step back and look at the broader picture, we will see they likely forged a friendship through the sharing of hardships and the bearing of testimony that edified, strengthened, and lifted one another. I think Mary and Elisabeth felt the reach of God through each other. They were the only two women in the world who could understand each other's calling and burden—with perfect love and perfect empathy. One carried the Son of God who would save us all from sin and oppression, and the other carried His personal Elias who sacrificed his life while paving the way for anyone willing to come unto Christ.

Elisabeth was barren, and yet Zacharias remained at her side, although the option for divorce due to her barrenness was his privilege under Jewish law (see Deuteronomy 24:1–4). As if the directive for divorce was not enough, feminine infertility was seen as a sign of divine disfavor, which means Elisabeth endured undue hardships and negative social stigmas along with immense heartache during her childless years (see Deuteronomy 7:12–14). After she learned she was pregnant, Elisabeth may have likened her miracle to other ancient pious women like Sarah, Rachel, and Hannah, who endured great affliction in their barrenness and after God came to them, they too were blessed with miracle pregnancies. During the five months she remained hidden in her pregnancy, she allowed herself to heal and finally rejoice in the little bundle growing inside of her, which she testified was a healing balm needed for all those wounds she obtained in her childless years (see Luke 1:24–25).

Young Mary also had a negative stigma to overcome. She was only espoused to Joseph, not married, and suddenly, she was pregnant. If her day was anything like our day, rumors and hurtful speculation regarding her pregnancy circled her little town. As Mary's womb started to grow, she no doubt endured negative attention from family and community members not willing to believe her miraculous story. Adding to the complication, biblical scholars say Mary was probably fourteen, as young as an eighth-grader today, which means her capacity to explain the heavenly manifestation may have been difficult due to a lack of mortal experience. Even Joseph was affected by the rumors and privately contemplated breaking the espousal (see Matthew 1:18–19). The Lord soothed Joseph's mind in a dream, told him not to put her away (divorce) and gave him an understanding of the miracle growing inside her (see Matthew 1:20–25).

After the Annunciation, I think Mary did not just travel to see Elisabeth. I think she *ran* to see Elisabeth and was completely enveloped in Elisabeth's loving embrace—for she was the only woman in the entire world who could connect to Mary's experience. In Elisabeth's arms, she could take rest from social ills and trust her heavenly encounter was honored with the highest reverence. By the time she reached Elisabeth, Mary had already considered the juxtaposition between her own lowly estate and the magnitude of the most holy calling God could bestow upon mankind—to be the mother of His only Begotten Son. Full of love and motivation to do the work given to her, she testified to Elisabeth, "My soul doth magnify the Lord, and my spirit hath rejoiced in God my Saviour. For he hath regarded the low estate of his handmaiden . . . [and] from henceforth all generations shall call me blessed" (Luke 1:46–48). Together, these two holy women rejoiced in full disclosure of their deepest fears and basked in each other's richest testimony.

Mary stayed with Elisabeth for three months (see Luke 1:56). In Mary's own divine manifestation, she was told Elisabeth was already six months pregnant (see Luke 1:36). You can do the math. It is very likely Elisabeth gave birth to her firstborn son while Mary tarried with her. What a glorious day Mary witnessed in Judea! Imagine their spiritual joy and elation to snuggle such a holy babe, John the Baptist. Imagine the confidence Mary gained to go and carry out the measure of her design, for shortly thereafter, "her days were accomplished that she should be delivered. And she brought forth her first-born son . . . which is Christ the Lord" (Luke 2:6–7, 11).

As women, let us rejoice together and honor Mary and Elisabeth for their mutual love, admiration, and fervent testimony. They allowed God's reach to lift each other as they contemplated and carried out their holy callings. Because of their willing obedience, it was made possible for all to come unto Jesus and to be redeemed by His grace.

We may never understand the extent of God's reach through woman to woman. President Russell M. Nelson said, "It would be impossible to measure the influence that . . . women have. . . . This has been true in every gospel dispensation since the days of Adam and Eve."[51] In the same article, he adds, "We need women who know how to make important things happen by their faith. . . . We need women who are devoted to shepherding God's children along the covenant path . . . women who know how to receive personal revelation . . . women who know how to call upon the power of heaven to protect and strengthen [other women]."[52]

I invite you to listen to the godly women in your life. Look around and see that God often reaches through them to come to you, and through you, to reach others. My sixteen-year-old daughter, Maddy, recently shared, "Women are the angels in other women's lives. It's up to us." I would add, sometimes . . . it's just between us.

A Divine Endowment

by Heather Farrell

*"And it shall come to pass afterward, that I will pour
out my spirit upon all flesh; and your sons and your
daughters shall prophesy, your old men shall dream
dreams, your young men shall see visions: And also
upon the servants and upon the handmaids in those
days will I pour out my spirit."*

—JOEL 2: 28-29

*S*everal years ago I was feeling really discouraged. I had little
demons sitting on my shoulders telling me that I was failing at everything. I knew it wasn't true, but I still couldn't combat the feelings of failure—that I was a failure with my kids, in my marriage, in my calling at
church, in my work, in my extended family, and in all my personal goals.
Worst of all, I felt like I was failing in my relationship with God and that
He was far away from me.

One evening, after a particularly hard day, my family was sitting
down to a very tense dinner when there was a knock at the door. I
opened it and saw our Relief Society president standing on the porch.
She smiled, reached out her arms to give me a hug, and said, "It is all
going to be okay." As she held me I felt a warm feeling of love flow
through my body, and I knew that God had not forgotten me. The
feeling made me start to cry. My crying took the Relief Society president by surprise, and she explained that she'd been driving home and
the thought came to her that she should go to my house, give me a
hug, and tell me that it was all going to be okay. She said she almost

hadn't come because it felt like a silly thing to do, but she'd come anyway. I couldn't explain through my tears but told her it was just what I had needed. Later I marveled at how my Relief Society president, so in tune with the Spirit, had brought the love and peace that I so desperately needed. She had been a messenger for God, bringing Him and His love to me.

Love is one of the most powerful of all the manifestations of God, because love is God. In 1 John 4:7–8, we learn that "everyone that loveth is born of God, and knoweth God . . . for God is love." God does not just *have* love, but He literally, in some cosmic way, *is* love. He is made of love, and when we show love for ourselves, our spouses, our children, our friends, and our neighbors, He is with us.

As women we have an incredible capacity to share love. President Russell M. Nelson taught, "Men can and often do communicate the love of Heavenly Father and the Savior to others. But women have a special gift for it—a divine endowment."[53] The word "endowment" means "that which is given or bestowed," and in a spiritual context the giver is God. Therefore, an endowment is something that God gives or bestows upon someone. For women the love that we feel for others, love that often comes so naturally to us is a gift, a divine power given to us from God.

Always to Be with Us

Elder Bruce R. McConkie wrote, "If the love of God abides in our souls, which love is a gift of God that comes by the power of the Holy Ghost, then God dwells in us. In some way beyond our comprehension, all of this is possible by the power of the Holy Ghost."[54] I think we sometimes discount the Holy Ghost, feeling that He is somehow the lesser member of the Godhead. One young woman I knew once described Him as "the second counselor in the Godhead." But this is not true.

In 2 Nephi 31:21 we learn that "this is the doctrine of Christ, and the only and true doctrine of the Father, and of the Son, and of the Holy Ghost, which is one God, without end." Joseph Smith, in *Lectures on Faith* taught, "These three are one; or, in other words, these three constitute the great, matchless, governing and supreme, power over all things; . . . and these three constitute the Godhead, and are one."[9]

As a member of the Godhead, the Holy Ghost, while a separate being, is still perfectly one with the Father and Jesus Christ, sharing the same power and purpose.[55] Elder Jeffery R. Holland said, "We believe these three divine persons constituting a single Godhead are united in purpose, in manner, in testimony, in mission. We believe Them to be filled with the same godly sense of mercy and love, justice and grace, patience, forgiveness, and redemption. I think it is accurate to say we believe They are one in every significant and eternal aspect imaginable *except* believing Them to be three persons combined in one substance."[56] The Holy Ghost is certainly not just the "second counselor" in the Godhead. He, in His unified role with the Father and the Son, *is* God, and the power that comes to us from Him is the power of God.

This is significant because when we make baptismal covenants we are given the gift of the Holy Ghost, which means we have the ability to have God with us as our constant companion. This promise is also repeated in the sacrament prayers where, after having made sacramental covenants, we are promised that we will "always have his spirit to be with us."[57] Who is the "he"? He is Jesus Christ. We are given the gift to have Jesus Christ, God, with us *always*, every moment of our lives. It is an astounding gift— one that I know I do not fully appreciate or even fully understand.

I once taught a Relief Society lesson on the Holy Ghost, and the discussion went a little off topic. In an attempt to bring the lesson back on track I began to bear my testimony of the Holy Ghost and said how even though I had never seen the Holy Ghost I knew who He was. I told the sisters that if He was to walk through the door of the Relief Society room right then, I would recognize Him because I had felt His presence almost every day of my life.

As I said those words the sisters went silent, and the most fantastic feeling came over the room. It felt as if someone, a strong divine presence, had literally just stepped into the Relief Society room. The feeling was so palpable that I turned my head toward the door of the room, fully expecting to see someone standing there. Describing it in words fails to convey the realness and nearness of that divine presence, but it was incredible. I realized that day that the Holy Ghost is real and that He can manifest Himself to us in real but unseen ways. God, especially in the form of the Holy Ghost, is with us much more often than we realize.

Gifts of the Spirit

Through the power given us by the Holy Ghost we have the ability to do great things. When Jesus ascended into heaven He promised His disciples that all those who believed in Him and were baptized would be given gifts and powers that would help them build His kingdom (see Mark 16:14–18). In Doctrine and Covenants 46 the Lord outlined what some of these powers are and specified that "to every man [and woman] is given a gift by the Spirit of God" (verse 11).

Some of these gifts are magnificent and pronounced, like the ability to be healed and to heal others, while other gifts, while equally as powerful, are more subtle, like the ability to believe, or having great faith. Yet no matter what the gift, dramatic or subtle, they all come to us through the power of the Holy Ghost.

In a 1975 *Ensign* article, Lane Johnson, wrote,

> God the Father is the ultimate repository of all intelligence, or, in other words, "light and truth" (D&C 93:36); Jesus Christ, the First-born, who became a god in the premortal existence, the Father's steward over his creations, is the one source of light for us as individuals; and the Holy Ghost is the "gatekeeper," as it were, the dispenser of light to us according to worthiness and ability to receive it.
>
> Gifts of the Spirit come to us in the form of pure intelligence or knowledge, transferred "in the abstract" (that is, spirit to spirit) through the Holy Ghost (*Teachings of the Prophet Joseph Smith*, p. 355), to enlighten our minds, open the eyes of our understanding, and manifest themselves as special abilities, skills, or capacities for understanding.[58]

When it comes to gifts of the Spirit, sometimes as women we may wonder what we are "allowed" to do without overstepping into the realm of the priesthood. This is a worthy concern, as honoring and respecting the priesthood brings power and protection into our lives. We also do not want to fall into the trap of using the gifts we have been given in wicked ways. Satan is always eager to ensnare God's saints into the misuse of their spiritual gifts for his own diabolical purposes. So it is important that as we discover the gifts we have been given, that we strive to be humble and prayerful about how to use them. We need to be sensitive to the Spirit, listening for His guiding voice to help us know how and when our gifts should be used and shared.

One of the spiritual gifts I have been given is the ability to teach. At times when I teach the right words, ideas, and messages come easily and quickly to my mind. When I put aside what I want to say and focus on what the Spirit is telling me to say, I have a beautiful experience. I feel carried away by the Spirit and feel a burning in my heart. I know that what I have said is true and that the Holy Ghost is working through me to convey the truth of those words to others. Yet there are other times when the Holy Ghost tells me *not* to say or do something, but I do it anyway because I want to, and then I discover that my gift is gone. In those cases my teaching is not anything remarkable; it lacks the power that only the Holy Ghost can bring.

As we are humble and prayerful in the use of our spiritual gifts, they will get stronger and our ability to bless others through the power of God will increase. Our prophet, Russell M. Nelson, has been encouraging women to develop and use our spiritual gifts. He said, "My dear sisters, you have special spiritual gifts and propensities. . . . I urge you, with all the hope of my heart, to pray to understand your spiritual gifts—to cultivate, use, and expand them, even more than you ever have. You will change the world as you do so."[59] The ability to work by the power of the Holy Ghost is power that is available to every member of Christ's church, male and female.

Charity Never Faileth

In his first letter to the Corinthians the Apostle Paul wrote about gifts of the Spirit. In 1 Corinthians 12 he outlined many gifts available to members of the Church, specifying they were "given by the spirit" (verse 8). Interestingly, right after this chapter about spiritual gifts we get 1 Corinthians 13, Paul's beautiful sermon about charity. In our Bibles these verses are broken into chapters, making them feel like they are separate, but in Paul's original letter, the chapter on spiritual gifts and charity would have flowed naturally into one another. Paul's sermon on charity is just an extension of his chapter on spiritual gifts. In fact, chapter 13 begins with Paul telling us that though we have "the gift of prophecy, and understand all mysteries, and all knowledge, and have all faith" that unless we have charity we are "nothing" (verse 2). Charity is the greatest of all spiritual gifts.

Paul tells us that "charity never faileth" and that it embodies a plethora of virtues: it suffers long, is kind, doesn't envy, is not puffed up, does not behave in an unseemly manner, is not easily provoked, and does not seek out evil. Moroni, who also wrote about gifts of the Spirit in the Book of Mormon, also ended his description of spiritual gifts by ending with charity, stating that it is "the pure love of Christ" (Moroni 10:18).

In fact, charity is one of the ultimate displays of God's power because charity *is* God. He is the one thing that "never faileth," the one thing in the universe that is constant, secure, and unchangeable. Without Him, without His love and condescension toward us, we are nothing. With Him we are everything, and, as Jesus taught, "With God all things are possible" (Matthew 19:26).

As women we have a special connection to charity. The motto of the Relief Society, God's organization for women, is "Charity Never Faileth." President Spencer W. Kimball said, "Women, so often, are charity personified."[60] This personification of women and charity does not mean that men do not also possess this gift, but I think it captures an important eternal truth, that the mission that God has given women, and which is magnified through the Relief Society, is to be ambassadors for God, carrying His love—carrying Him—to the four corners of the earth and His light to the darkest reaches of the earth.

The following story about Lucy Mack Smith illustrates beautifully the power that women have to work miracles and do great things through the righteous exercise of our love. Lucy's sons Hyrum and the Prophet Joseph Smith were marching with Zion's Camp toward Independence, Missouri, when, as Joseph related:

> Soon after arriving at the point of destination, the cholera broke out in our midst; the brethren were so violently attacked that it seemed impossible to render them any assistance. They immediately sent for us to lay hands on them, but we soon discovered that this, also, was a judgment from the Almighty; for, when we laid our hands upon them, in the name of the Lord, the disease immediately fastened itself upon us and in a few minutes we were in awful agony. We made signals to each other and left the house in order to join in prayer to God that he would deliver us from this dreadful influence; but, before we could get to a sufficient distance from the house to be secure from interruption, we were hardly able to stand upon our feet, and we feared that we should die.

These faithful men of God, just recently ordained with the priesthood and still trying to grasp its full ability, had been unable to cure others with its power. They were confused and discouraged, and in danger of succumbing to the disease themselves. Joseph continued,

> We succeeded in getting a few steps further, and then fell upon our knees and cried unto the Lord that he would deliver us from

this awful calamity, but we arose worse than before. We kneeled down the second time, and when we commenced praying the cramp seized us, gathering the cords in our arms and legs in bunches and operating equally severe throughout our system. We still besought the Lord, with all our strength, to have mercy upon us, but all in vain. It seemed as though the heavens were sealed against us, and that every power that could render us any assistance was shut within its gates. . . .

After praying some time the cramp began to release its hold; and, in a short time, Hyrum sprang to his feet and exclaimed, "Joseph, we shall return to our families. I have had an open vision, in which I saw mother kneeling under an apple tree; and she is even now asking God, in tears, to spare our lives, that she may again behold us in the flesh. The Spirit testifies, that her prayers, united with ours, will be answered." "Oh, my mother!" said Joseph, "how often have your prayers been the means of assisting us when the shadows of death encompassed us.[61]

It was the love of their mother, praying with faith for the safe return of her sons, that healed Joseph and Hyrum. When the heavens seemed sealed and as Joseph said, "Every power that could render us any assistance was shut within its gates," it was the love and faith of a woman, combined with that of her sons, that opened the heavens and poured down divine power.

Sometimes in the Church women feel inferior to men because we are not ordained to the priesthood. We may feel like God has not given us power, not given us anything equal to the priesthood ordination that men receive. Yet I think that women's ability to use our spiritual gifts, which come to us through the Holy Ghost, gives us an enormous amount of power. I think this is especially true for the gift of charity, a divine endowment given to women, which enables us to access the depth of God's power and wield it righteously.

I had an experience that, in my mind, is similar to that of Lucy Mack Smith's. I was at a junior high wrestling tournament, watching my son Asher wrestle. Usually Asher wrestles on the varsity team, but that week he had been beaten out of his varsity position by another boy on his team so he was wrestling on the JV mat for this meet. The boy he was wrestling was much less experienced, and Asher pinned him within seconds. After they shook hands the boy from the other team went over to the bleachers, curled up in the fetal position, and began to cry.

I was sitting across the gym and saw it all happen. I could tell this boy had a rough life, and it broke my heart to think that my son had, although very unintentionally, made it harder. I felt my heart fill with love for the boy. I bowed my head and said a silent prayer that this boy would feel God's love for him, that he would know that someone cared about him. As I prayed I filled my heart with love and then "pushed" it, kind of like a Care Bear, across the gym toward the boy. I was amazed when right away, as if he had felt the love I had pushed at him, the boy uncurled, sat up, and wiped his eyes. It seemed sort of miraculous, so I tried again.

The boy had sat alone the whole meet. I'd never even seen one of his teammates glance his way. So I prayed that someone would notice him and go to him. Again I tried to "push" my love his way and was amazed when again, almost immediately, a boy on the other side of the bleachers stood up, walked over, and put his arm around the struggling boy. By this time I was amazed and feeling incredibly powerful. Had I just done all that? Or was it some cosmic coincidence?

All I knew is that my heart had been filled with love for that lonely boy, I had prayed, asking God to share my love, and it had happened. Somehow God had sent love, flying across the junior high gym, from my heart into the hearts of others, and someone had been healed. It felt like a miracle.

I think that if we as women want to rise to our full potential, we must first comprehend the magnitude of the gifts and power that God has given us. He has endowed us with His love. It is a real power, one that has the ability to influence and change the world in very real ways. Best of all, God's love is bottomless, and we can never run out of it, no matter how much we give away.

It is beautiful to remember that, in what is the most glorious of all the times when God has come to women, Jesus entrusted Himself to Mary, a young woman with no wealth, no status, and no worldly power. He, the all-powerful creator of the universe, came to earth as a meek and humble baby, to be cared for, loved, and taught by a woman.

In fact, when the angel of the Lord showed Nephi the vision of the tree of life, the first thing he did to help Nephi understand the meaning of the tree was to show him a vision of Mary holding Jesus in her arms. "Knowest thou the meaning of the tree?" the angel asked Nephi after Nephi had seen Mary and Jesus together. "Yea," Nephi replied, "it is the love of God" (1 Nephi 11:21–22). The most supreme example that the angel could give of the love of God was that of Jesus Christ coming to earth, embraced in the arms of a woman.

God has endowed women with charity, the ability to access Him and His endless wealth of power. He has given us Himself. The love we feel for others *is* Him, and when we have open and receptive hearts, He can fill us with His love, a power that "never faileth." Through the righteous exercise of our spiritual gifts, women have the ability to change, bless, and heal the world. God is truly never far from us, because in the face of each person who loves, we find God.

God Is Hope

by Jen Mabray

*I will not leave you comfortless: I will
come to you.*

—JOHN 14:18

$\mathcal{I}$f you read this whole book, thank you. I'm glad you're here. But if you feel like the stories and scriptures describing how God comes to women is not enough, or you feel you have not had spiritual experiences, take heart. I admire your honest introspection of self. The possibilities for God's communication to us are not limited to our own understanding, and at times His ways can be easily clouded by mortal challenges that prohibit clarity of mind and heart. Sometimes the dark fog of depression and anxieties, feelings of hopelessness, and lack of purpose accompany women. If these are your days right now, this chapter is for you. I want to make my remarks personal and call you my sister.

Dear Sister, I sense behind your smile you struggle mightily, and words fall short to explain the depth of your feelings. I know sometimes you feel a sense of heaviness in your arms and legs, and daily breath can be exhausting. I understand some days you feel hauntingly alone, even in the company of friends and loved ones, and like a vulture who circles the weak and dying, guilt is your constant companion. I imagine you plead in your closets to reach God, yet you feel the ceiling absorbs your reaching before it penetrates heaven. I know your pillow soaks up your thick and salty tears at night. I understand how crucial it is for your soul to feel emotionally secure and to hear real expressions of love and peace.

No doubt you know that our Lord Jesus Christ was not a stranger to despair. Isaiah's words echoed in G.F. Handel's *Messiah* offer a chilling depiction of the humiliation and suffering of our Lord: "Surely, surely He hath borne our griefs, and carried our sorrows" (Isaiah 53:4). For this reason alone, I believe He will never dismiss our cries, our feelings, or our needs and count them as insignificant.

Because of His experience and His eternal role, our Savior Jesus Christ beckons for you to come unto Him. He calls to you in the darkness, "Come unto me, all ye that labour and are heavy laden, and I will give you rest. Take my yoke upon you, and learn from me; for I am gentle and humble in heart: and ye will find rest for your souls. For my yoke is easy, and my burden is light" (Matthew 11:28–30, NIV). To this end . . . I hope, dear sister, that hope is not lost.

The irony of the "yoke" passage has always held my attention. A yoke is a wooden shoulder-beam used to link oxen or work animals together as one. Although their power together is stronger than the power of one, each animal still carries a portion of the heavy burden. Christ tells us His yoke is easy, and His burden is light. This seems to suggest, then, that maybe the yoke of Christ is not equally balanced, as it must be when two oxen are yoked.

Why, when we feel we have no more to give, does He ask us to come unto Him? Are those not the times we need Him to *come to us?* It seems easy to arrive at the understanding that everything good takes effort. Parenting takes effort. Education takes effort. Gaining a testimony and witness of God takes effort. So too, coming to Christ to take His yoke upon us requires effort. My husband shared that when he was a teenager, he asked his mother how to help someone who no longer had any desire to do anything. Her answer remains with him today. She explained the importance of loving someone enough to walk with them, to lift their burden, and at times to literally put on their shoes and carry them until they have the strength to do for themselves what previously seemed impossible. The Savior loves us enough to walk with us, lift, us, and carry us, which is part of the blessing of taking His yoke upon us. But before we take His yoke, we have to come to Him.

With permission, I would like to share a small snippet of Sarah Frei's story. On July 30, 2020, Sarah was hit by a drunk driver and had to undergo a double amputation of both of her legs at mid-thigh, and is now a T11 paraplegic.[62] I have followed Sarah on social media throughout her hospital stay and parts of her recovery, and watched so many people do exactly what my husband's mother said. Loving caretakers and family members literally walked *for* Sarah, lifted her, and carried her. On November 13, 2020, she was able to accomplish a monumental feat and sit up for the first time without help. When I talked with Sarah, she was bubbly and bright and testified, "I have come so close to the Savior throughout this experience." Indeed she has come close to the Lord! She has worked so hard, and her strength and testimony are reaching thousands across the world through social media.

I mention Sarah's story to draw a parallel between her ongoing recovery and coming unto Christ. He says to come unto Him, but for some that might feel truly impossible due to a lack in faith, trust, and even clarity of purpose. Sarah is now home with her family, but she needs consistent care from her doctors and physical therapists. Although doctors may call upon us from time to time in our homes, in America we tend to travel *to* the doctor, no matter our condition. Despite her growing independence, just to go to the doctor requires many steps, including patience and hard work to sit up, balance, and safely scooch over into her wheelchair. In this parallel, the Savior is her doctor, and Sarah's efforts to come to the doctor parallel the struggle required to come unto Jesus. Additionally, Sarah has to trust that the struggle to sit up to go to the doctor is worth it. Her trust in her doctor's care mirrors the trust we must have in our Savior, the trust we must give Him despite our own lack of faith and clarity of purpose. As Sarah continues to practice her new skills, she learns to trust that no effort is wasted. The same is true for anyone. As we practice coming unto Christ, we will gain confidence that our struggles and efforts will not be wasted and will be for our benefit and growth.

I have thought about my second example for a long time. Many years ago, a friend of mine shared she had two brothers who passed away from muscular dystrophy. One day, during a spiritual conversation she asked me how Christ could understand muscular dystrophy if He had never had that debilitating disease. Her question stumped me, and I asked if I could take some time to return to my house to study, pray, and think.

As I studied, I focused particularly on Christ's Atonement. I wanted to know how He understands our burdens and infirmities. I felt like I could answer the why: because He loves us. The concept of His love made sense to me. But I wanted to know *how*. We believe that when Christ was in Gethsemane, He began the Atonement for our sins and felt our infirmities (see Matthew 26:36–46, Mark 14:32–50, Luke 22:39–46). Through revelation we are told He descended below all things so He could comprehend all things (see D&C 88:6). The word "descend" captured me, and I felt the answer was somewhere in its concept. Exactly what and how did He descend?

We believe Christ triumphed over *all* things, after His descent of *all* things. Through His incomprehensible journey accompanied with agony, darkness, and a terrible exaction of divine will, He felt the full range of human suffering of mortality and death, which gave Him perfect empathy and an eternal knowledge of how to conquer *anything*. To me, the concept of descent was the key! If muscular dystrophy represented a pit for humankind, Christ descended into the pit of muscular dystrophy to gain experience with the hellish powers of its all-encompassing grasp. However, the scripture says, "He descended below all things." This means He did not just hit rock-bottom, He went *even lower*. Follow me in this imagery. Christ descended to the place with muscular dystrophy that receives *no light*, and grappled with its damning challenges. In His ascent from the pit, He reached His Father, even the right hand of God, and opened the blessings of justice, mercy, and restitution for all. Thus He comprehended *every* aspect of the disease. But this is not all, He did not just descend below one oppression. He descended below the powers of sin and death, depression and anxiety, abuse and betrayal, sickness and pain—every heartache and every disappointment. Christ *descended below our struggles* so He could understand and make restitution for *all*.

Dear Sister, remember the verse in Matthew, where He petitioned us to come unto Him, to take His yoke upon us (Matthew 11:28–30). He says His yoke is easy and light. If we feel we are not strong enough to come unto Christ, remember just as Sarah's efforts to sit up are not wasted, so too, our efforts to come unto Him will not be wasted. Because He descended below all things and has the strength of heaven to lift, He has the capacity to carry our burdens. I believe this is true, which means our job is to *trust* Him.

What If All Feeling Seems to Be Gone?

Although I do not suffer from clinical depression, I have had two very dark, lengthy seasons that have literally inhibited my ability to feel or hear the Spirit, or really *to feel anything*. Jesus says, "Behold, I stand at the door, and knock: if any man[woman] hear my voice, and open the door, I will come in to him [her] and sup with him [her] and he [she] with me" (Revelation 3:20). The darkness of my depression and a loss of interest in life or activity prevented me from "hearing any knock." I have almost no recollection of God coming to me in those times, not because He didn't come, but because *I could not* feel Him. And for a time, the only way I could bring myself to *come unto Him,* was to cling to my knowledge and beliefs, both of which testify He does not leave us comfortless during seasons of trouble and doubt.

Sometimes, I collect passages of Christ's words, recorded in scripture, to help break a cycle of what I call "mortal stagnancy," or the feeling of no progressive movement. I call them scriptural melodies. It's not new scripture or a new interpretation of His words; it's just a collection of His words arranged in a way that speaks to me. My favorite melody begins like this:

Dear Daughter,
> Why weepest thou? Whom seekest thou?
> Rejoice in hope; [be] patient in tribulation; [continue] in constant prayer.
> I tell you the truth; It is expedient for you that I go away . .
> But behold, I will not leave you comfortless: I will come to you . . . yet a little while . . . ye will see me.[63]

If you have days you do not want to get out of bed, or cannot seem to bring yourself to be present in family life or activity, when it is difficult to feel the Spirit or you feel low in your self-esteem, use His words to create a personal dialogue. It is possible for you to create something that will touch your heart when little else can. Remember, even the Savior cried out in agony while on the cross, "Eli, Eli, lama sabachthani? (My God, my God, why hast thou forsaken me?)" (Matthew 27:46).[64] He too felt the suffocating void that envelops us when we cannot feel, cannot hear, or cannot experience God. The Young Women theme affirms, "We are daughters of our Heavenly Parents, who love us and we love them."[65]

Loving parents do not leave their children comfortless or walk out on them during times of distress and discouragement. If you have ever personally cared for someone in the middle of a difficult trial, you as the caretaker may notice that the one you care for has not the capacity to notice that you are there. However, you are there and doing all you can to help. I think of a dedicated nurse who comes in to check on their patient after surgery. The patient may be incoherent, yet their needs are closely watched and attended to. Our Heavenly Parents are the same. Although we may not feel the presence of God at all times, lean on your previous understanding and confirmations during times when you could feel, and know that God attends to our needs and watches closely over His children. All the previous stories in this book testify that He comes. With all the evidence before us, we have to believe that He comes no matter what . . . even when we cannot see, feel, or experience Him.

Last, if we feel we might misunderstand His voice or are blinded by the traumas of mortality so we cannot see Him, may I suggest we look backward instead of forward. In April 1829, the Lord told Oliver Cowdery, who struggled with doubt and longed for clarification of God's favor, "If you desire a further witness, cast your mind upon the night that you cried unto me in your heart. . . . Did I not speak peace to your mind concerning the matter? What greater witness can you have than from God?" (D&C 6:22–24). If we apply this counsel and look backward when our current situation feels bleak, we might find the strength to press on. Let me illustrate this with a very personal story.

On February 22, 2016, I stepped out of a meeting room in a morgue in Fort Worth, Texas, where my siblings were discussing burial options for my dad. An older man with white hair in a grey-brown tweed suit approached me while I sat alone, crying, on a sofa. The man told me he worked as a helper and asked if he could sit next to me. I was startled by his forwardness, but he set my heart and mind immediately at ease with his gentle nature. He introduced himself as Charlie and asked if I wanted some water. Nodding, I followed him like a lost puppy to a kitchenette, where we sat quietly across a small table from each other. He broke the silence when he said, "We all have to watch loved ones pass through the veil."

"The veil?" I responded.

Did the stranger just say veil? Perhaps sensing my surprise to hear that word outside a religious discussion, he smiled and asked me if I would share my faith with him. I agreed and conjured into words a simple testimony of Jesus Christ despite my heavy heart. After each phrase I uttered, the old man offered a nod and said, "Mmm hmm." When I finished speaking he said matter-of-factly, "That is correct." The thought crossed my mind that he was mocking me, so I again sat quietly. He then elaborated on my words and spoke boldly about a plan the Lord has for all His children to return home to Him. Tears streamed from my swollen eyes as I recognized peaceful doctrinal truths I have believed all my life. Piercing my heart-wrenching despair, the man shared that he, too, had experienced many challenging days and discouraging situations. Tenderly, he shared he knew my dad's body was in another room. I wondered if he knew my dad had just taken his own life.

Charlie asked if he could take me for a drive around the cemetery grounds. I followed him again as he walked to the front desk, picked up a set of keys, and led me to a golf cart. Outside he explained, "I think I can drive one of these things. I'm sure they won't mind."

With one eyebrow raised and slightly concerned, I climbed into the front seat next to the old man, and he drove me around the cemetery and mausoleum. Sunlight passed through the century-old oak trees, dappling the marble headstones and manicured lawn with golden beams. He noticed and commented on my admiration of the light pouring through the trees and asked if he could show me a place in the cemetery that he felt "always had special light." Under a large oak tree with wide sweeping branches that reached out over the expanse of many graves, the light touched the ground and was indeed special. I felt a certain peace and thought, *Maybe my dad would be happy to rest here.*

He returned the golf cart and then he asked me if I wanted to play the piano in the morgue chapel. I silently wondered how he knew I could play but dismissed the notion. He poked his head around a corner and turned it sideways as he looked down a long hallway and said, "I don't think they will mind. It's okay." Feeling comfortable and also a bit strange with him sitting next to me, I played for a few moments, bringing yet another measure of peace, a soothing balm to my wounded heart.

My siblings were still in their meeting somewhere in the building, and I felt I had regained a moment of strength to return to that conversation. I told Charlie I did not know where they were, and he replied, "I do. I'll take you to them." This time I walked beside him as he guided me to one of the many closed doors down a large corridor. I smiled at him the best I could and slipped inside, taking my chair next to my older brother. When the gentlemen leading the discussion asked if we wanted to select a plot, I shared that a man named Charlie showed me a quiet place I found peaceful near a large oak tree. He replied, "Charlie? Hmm, not sure who that is. But no matter, we will go look at that plot together." I never saw Charlie again. When I returned to the morgue later that week, I looked for and inquired about Charlie. There was no Charlie. There never was a Charlie.

From time to time, I have considered whether or not Charlie really did work at the morgue. Maybe I have remembered his name wrong, and that is why no one knew of him. Thankfully, the effects of trauma did not remove my memory of his kindness. Today, when I look back, I offer gratitude to Heavenly Father for a sweet old man who found a way to momentarily penetrate the barrier of my grief and soothe my soul. I choose to believe Charlie was heaven-sent during a most desperate and trying time.

The trial of losing my dad to suicide plunged me into a spiraling darkness, the likes of which I have never been able to put to words. For the better part of two years, I did not know how to yoke myself with Christ and come unto Him, and I wondered if He came to me. I held an image in my mind that I was lost at sea and pleaded for God to come and take the helm of my little boat. On my starboard side, monstrous waves representing the original trauma and unrelenting challenges thereafter threatened to capsize me. On my port side, I felt threatened by the mind-numbing doldrums of depression and stagnant progression. Luckily, I stayed in my "little boat," clinging to my beliefs, to previous experiences with God, and my scriptural studies. I do not mean to paint a beautiful picture here. I truly felt threatened by the anguish of suicide and literally *clung* to my little boat. I believed God could take the helm and safely navigate both waters, but until clarity of mind and strength of being slowly returned, I struggled to recognize whether or not He was there.

Dear Sister, if you also find yourself in a season wherein you cannot feel, take a moment to recall your past experiences. It may seem so basic to remember and cling a past positive experience, but a "return to the basics" during difficult times might be a solution to help you push through your challenges until you can feel that God comes to you again. Although, I do not think our challenges in mortality will cease, I do believe the Savior knows how to navigate all the difficult waters of our lives, both present and future. Plead with Him to "take the helm of your little boat." While in difficult waters, look back on previous experiences and cling to what you know to be true—even the testimony and conviction of others. It might just help you to stay the course through your present challenges.

When Hope Is Not Enough

God uses all kinds of mediums to come to His daughters, to touch our hearts, to heal our pain, to lift our souls, to show His love. However, there is still one pressing concern . . . a loss of hope. Often scriptural accounts and experiences from other women, and our own personal experiences, can give us great confidence in God and keep hope alive. However, there are times and situations that truly make us feel hopeless. What do you do when hope is not enough?

Ethel Smith, wife of Joseph Fielding Smith, suffered from an illness that left her confused and frustrated. Sometimes she was plunged into the depths of depression and at other times her mind raced beyond control forcing her exhausted body to do more and more. Regardless of blessings, hospitalizations, prayers, and the continual love and support of her family, the suffering did not cease.[66] Scholars now know that Ethel struggled with mental illness, a concept that was still in its infancy in her day. Her husband penned a poem in a letter in 1924, while he was away on church business, hoping it would give her the strength of mind to press on. The words of his poem are especially poignant to describe heavy burdens:

> Does the journey seem long
> The path rugged and steep?
> Are there briars and thorns on the way?
> Do sharp stones cut your feet
> As you struggle to rise
> To the heights thru the heat of the day?
>
> Is your heart faint and sad,
> Your soul weary within,
> As you toil 'neath your burden of care?
> Does the load heavy seem
> You are forced now to lift?
> Is there no one your burden to share?
>
> Let your heart be not faint
> Now the journey's begun;
> There is One who still beckons to you.
> So look upward in joy
> And take hold of his hand;
> He will lead you to heights that are new.[67]

Despite his best efforts and the care of others, Ethel's inner burden became worse, and she suffered terribly during the final four years of her life. Her debilitating illness sadly overcame her and she died on August 26, 1937. Scientists know that mental illness does not discriminate between age, gender, social status, or work ethic. It touches women who are close to God, strong in their convictions, and who have treasured accounts of when God came to them. Additionally, family members and friends are often at a loss of how to help their loved one during the lowest points of no hope. Just as cancer can beat the strongest soul, so too can mental illness. Remember, Christ descended below cancer to be able to empathize with the struggles and make restitution for the pain and missed opportunities. The all-encompassing descent of Jesus' Atonement also applies to mental illness and a loss of hope.

Sometimes in the face of difficult challenges, hope is all we have. Jewish prisoner Seren Tuval Bernstein was one of seventy-nine Romanian women sent to Ravensbrück, the largest concentration camp in the German Reich for women during World War II. It is calculated that more than 50,000 women perished at Ravensbrück from gunshots, disease, starvation, exposure, rape, scientific experiments, exhaustion, and the gas chambers.[68] Her memoir, *The Seamstress*, reveals a truly terrifying story that leaves the reader in reverent awe of her courage and grit to survive despite the horror she experienced.[69]

Seren held on to a hope that she would one day be liberated. However, one of Seren's bunkmates, Lily, had her glasses smashed during a fist-blow to her face by a camp guard and lost hope. Lily knew her days would soon end if she was found lingering on the job due to her eyesight. During the final weeks of Lily's life, Seren told Lily to hold on to her arm everywhere they went. Without her glasses, Lily could only make out fuzzy shapes and hazy colors.[70] Seren led Lily daily to places of relative safety tucked behind other female workers, giving Lily the ability and time to feel her work since she could not see. Lily did pass away shortly thereafter, and although the sadness felt overwhelming, Seren turned to her other two bunkmates, Esther and Ellen, and did her best to bandage their bleeding hope.

Seren once exclaimed, "I refuse to die."[71] In the most difficult weeks prior to liberation, they survived on yellowed grass Seren foraged from under a large board in the courtyard. Each time she tried to gather grass for food, she was subject to open gunfire by the remaining guards in their abandoned camp who decided to exterminate as many prisoners as they could so no one could testify what happened in the camp.[72] After what was coined a "death march" for the remaining female prisoners to another camp, a male prisoner and nephew to Seren, named Joseph, snuck food and bandages he had hidden in his clothes to Seren when he heard she was close to him. He told Seren to hold on, that it would be over soon. He pleaded, "You must believe, Seren!"

"Don't worry! I'm going to live!" Seren stammered. "I have to see how it all ends. I'll be here on the day when it's finally over. Maybe not the day after—but on that day I'll be alive."[73] Upon liberation in April 1945, American soldiers found Seren, Esther, and Ellen and took them to a large make-shift hospital-tent for care. Esther and Ellen were whisked away on stretchers and a soldier carried Seren. She recalled, "I felt myself being lifted up in two arms. I opened my eyes. One of the American soldiers was carrying me. I closed my eyes again [and] drops of water began splashing on my cheeks and running down my neck. *Is it raining again?* I thought. . . . Then I realized that the soldier carrying me was crying, his tears falling on my face."[74]

Seren weighed forty-four pounds at the end of the war.[75] Although Seren's body never fully recovered from the abuses she received in the death camps, she lived many decades after the war with a strength unmatched by most women around her.

What do we do, though, if we do not have the internal strength of Seren and feel we've lost hope? What if physical suffering does not end in this life? If you find yourself asking these questions, know you are not alone. Men and women have suffered from every nation, and every land, and from every era since Adam and Eve. Sometimes I wonder about the first heartache, the first potential loss of hope, when Eve laid her precious Abel into the grave. I wonder if she experienced the suffocation of grief, the fogginess of depression, and the depths of disappointment.

Dr. Martin Luther King Jr. said, "We must accept finite disappointment, but never lose finite hope."[76] Some of you reading this chapter will connect with the reality of really tough experiences and also know the power of severe trials. If we are willing, severe trials and affliction can sanctify us and bring us closer to God. Conversely, if we are not careful, severe trials and affliction can draw us away from God and cause us to cease reaching for Him. This is a reality we must fight.

Once, as written in the gospel of Mark, a father without hope, answers, or relief from a terrible trial with his son, came to Jesus. The father explained to Jesus that Jesus' apostles tried to give a blessing to the boy, but to no avail. In utter despair, the father pleaded with Jesus, "If thou canst do *any thing*, have compassion on us, and help *us*" (Mark 9:17–22, emphasis added). Jesus' answer was a beckoning call to the hopeless to continue to reach for God. He said, "If thou canst believe, all things are possible to him that believeth" (Mark 9:23). As I picture the imagery of the situation, I see a vulnerable father who quickly realized in his weakness, he could not escape his imperfect faith and loss of hope for things outside his control. But still he fought to come close to God as witnessed by his search for Jesus' help. In what might be some of the most poignant words ever to be canonized, the father offered a piercing cry, "Lord, I believe, help thou mine unbelief" (Mark 9:24). If in your severe trials, mortal vulnerabilities speak louder than your faith, follow the example of the heartbroken father and reach out to God. You may even think to cry out in prayer, "Lord, I believe, help me with my unbelief" (Luke 11:11–13, NIV).

As Dr. Martin Luther King Jr. said, we must never lose hope. I would add that we must never lose our faith and trust in God, and remember that God comes to women in all times, and in all places.[77] This does not mean only in happy times and in super-tidy spaces. It means all. We must not allow the concept that God comes to women to perish from our consciousness. God comes to us in so many ways—through words, thoughts, feelings, and experiences. We must believe that our loving Father in Heaven seeks to bless us and that hope emanates from His Son! Just before the horrific trial of the crucifixion, Jesus taught, "In the world ye shall have tribulation" (John 16:33). He followed with what has to be one of the most glorious promises of hope: "But be of good cheer; I have overcome the world" (John 16:33).

Dear Sister, be of good cheer, and let your heart believe that He has overcome all doubt, all pain, all infirmities, all loss, all heartache. If we yoke ourselves with Him, remember, His yoke is easy and His burden is light.

Closing

Behold, I stand at the door, and knock: if any [woman] hear my voice, and open the door, I will come in to [her], and will sup with [her], and [she] with Me.

—REVELATION 3:20

*W*hen Heather and I decided to write this book, we hoped and prayed that readers would see themselves somewhere in the stories, either in those from long ago, or in those that just happened yesterday and see that God really does come to women. Not only does He come to women, but He also champions women! He sees us, rejoices with us, talks and walks with us, and weeps with us. In a previous chapter, Heather said, "If we are constantly looking and listening for daily spiritual experiences, ones that come to us in the daily work of our lives, then we will find ourselves overflowing with spiritual experiences that keep our souls fed." I would add, if we look and listen for spiritual experiences, we will learn certain patterns of His communication and see He has come to us, and seeks each one of us still.

Recognition is one of the keys to divine manifestations. If we do not recognize Him, we may fail to hear His communication, or we may miss the "knock at the door." Thankfully, just like your sweet neighbor who continues to bring cookies, your best friend who keeps texting you silly memes late at night, or your sister who is always there no matter how long ago it was you spoke, God continues to call. If you missed the knock at the door, chances are, according to all His patterns and promises, He will come again.

God is close, even visible! Just consider the evidence found in sacred texts, the record of the personal experiences of the women you just read, and your own personal experiences we hope you recalled while reading this book. Additionally, we hope that you will take the time to record how and when God has spoken and visited you. There is a difference between journaling or posting about daily life and writing down your experiences with God. One is therapeutic, fun, and beneficial for your posterity to remember. The other is about holy preservation and mindful intent. Journaling your experiences with God will help you track God's pattern of communication to you, make you conscious of your inner dialogue with Him, and improve your perception of His presence.

Thankfully, men and women from antiquity recorded their sacred experiences. Thankfully, scriptural editors and redactors preserved those stories in our sacred canons. Many scriptural authors, like Samuel, Jeremiah, Malachi, the authors of the Gospels, Paul, and Mormon who authored the Book of Mormon, tell us their purpose was to bring souls to God and to preserve God's patterns of communication for generations to come. I am not suggesting we should add to recognized and respected canonized texts, but I am suggesting that if we record our experiences with God with the idea of holy preservation and mindful intent, then perhaps when the world is ready for the other half of its sacred encounters, it will be our privilege as women to bring forward a rich record of treasured accounts.

Dear Sister, we believe God comes to women. We believe He reserves time for His daughters, collectively and individually. We believe we are loved by Him, and it is our privilege to be blessed, found, lifted, taught, understood, and healed by Him. When you desire to meet with your Father in Heaven, we believe if you have not the capacity to commune with Him on the mountaintop, or the valley low, we offer our heartfelt testimony: God comes to women where they are.

—Jen Mabray and Heather Farrell

To Deepen Your Study

$\mathcal{L}$aurel Thatcher-Ulrich, a professor of history at Harvard, a Pulitzer Prize-winning writer, and a celebrated Latter-day Saint woman, wrote: "Most well-behaved women are too busy living their lives to think about recording what they do and too modest about their own achievements to think anybody else will care. . . . Women make history when they do the unexpected, when they create and preserve records and when later generations care."[78]

We hope that as you read this book memories of the ways in which God has visited and spoken to you have come to your mind. They may be big "mountaintop" experiences or small, simple experiences, but we hope that no matter what size they are you will take the time to write down the ways in which God has come to you. We promise you that future generations will be blessed and be grateful for anything you take time to record.

We have provided some empty pages in the back of this book for you to write down your experiences, but feel free to write them down in a personal journal or memory book too. We have also pulled questions from each of the chapters to help you deepen your study. We hope that these questions will inspire ideas and memories, and will help you delve into the scriptures to create a deeper and stronger relationship with Jesus Christ. He loves you and we hope that you learn to see that He comes to you more often than you realize.

Questions from *When You Can't Climb the Mountain*

1. Have you had an experience in your life, when, like Enos and the woman with the issue of blood, you have felt God tell you, "Thy faith hath made thee whole," either physically or spiritually? If so, how did your faith in Jesus Christ make that miracle possible?

2. When have you felt "separated" from God or from others? Did that experience bring you closer to God like it did for the woman with an issue of blood? Why or why not?

3. The phrase about "how beautiful upon the mountains are the feet of him that publisheth peace" is repeated several times throughout the scriptures (see Isaiah 52:7; 1 Nephi 13:37; Mosiah 12:21; 15:15–18; 3 Nephi 20:40; D&C 128:19). Take some time to read and study these scriptures and the context in which they were given. Why do you think this scripture is so often repeated? What does it mean to you?

Questions from *A Treasured Friendship*

1. What similarities between Jesus and Martha's friendship do you see between you and God?

2. What evidence have you seen that God uses friendship, love, and connection to touch our souls?

3. How does God seek a friendship with you? What types of commonalities do you share?

4. How do you take care of your friends and friendships?

5. Do you have a story of when a friend lovingly corrected you? How did it go?

6. When is a good time to invite a friend or friends and together learn more about God?

Questions from *Seeing God*

1. When God spoke to Hagar, He called her by name. This is a pattern in the scriptures, and many prophets have been called in similar ways. For example, when God spoke to Moses from the burning bush He called him by name saying, "Moses, Moses," to which Moses responded, "Here am I" (Exodus 3:4). How does knowing that God knows your name make your relationship with Him stronger? Have you ever had an experience where you ever felt God call your name?

2. In the New Testament there are several beautiful stories of women who are seen by Jesus Christ, even though they were not seeking His attention. Study the story of the widow of Nain in Luke 7:11–17 and the Woman with the Spirit of Infirmity in Luke 13:11–16. In what ways did Jesus see them? How do you know that God can see you?

3. When Hagar was in the wilderness, God asked her three questions: "Where did you come from? Where are you going? What troubles you?" Take time to answer and reflect on these questions in your own life. How might the answers to these questions guide and direct your life?

Questions from *God Waits for Us*

1. When is your *sixth hour*? Is there a time you step away because you do not fit in, or because you need a break from the company of others?

2. When has God sought to recover you from the shackles of negative social stigmas and cultural boundaries? How has He helped you to know that He is stronger than man's boundaries? Do you feel fully devoted to Him, or do the barriers get in between you?

3. Do you feel events in your past stand in the way of your devotion to God? If you have been hurt by someone, have you been able to learn to trust that God will not hurt you? What do you feel you need to overcome those hurts? Have you given yourself grace and time to heal? No matter the time needed?

4. Where do you feel you have access to *everlasting* water?

5. When has Christ testified to you of His divine mission?

6. Have you felt called by God to testify of Him after a particular experience?

Questions from *A Sacred Partnership*

1. What revelation or direction has God given you about your stewardship over your family, mortal and eternal? How did you know it was God directing you?

2. If you are not married or have been unable to have children, how has God helped you understand the eternal nature of your family? What direction or revelation has He given you that has helped you to see how you are assisting in His great work and glory?

3. In Moses 1:39 God told Moses, "For behold, this is my work and my glory—to bring to pass the immortality and eternal life of man." Take some time to study this story, the verse preceding this scripture, and the ones after, and reflect upon why God would tell this to Moses. How did knowing what God's plan was change him? How does knowing God's plan and your role in it change your perspective?

Questions from *Just between Us*

1. What does godly love and concern look like for you?

2. Who are the women in your life that God has asked you to help, love, and nurture?

3. What is the best part about reaching another woman in the name of God?

4. Who has reached you and made you feel that God sent her in His name?

5. Do you feel that God knows what you need? Can you write down what you feel you need from God?

Questions from *A Divine Endowment*

1. The gifts of the Spirit are listed in three places in the standard works: 1 Corinthians 12, Moroni 10, and Doctrine and Covenants 46. Read through these chapters, making notes about what is the same and what is different about them. Make a list of all the gifts you find and try to write down people in your life that exemplify each gift. Don't forget to include yourself!

2. How has the Relief Society, or your membership in Relief Society, helped you draw closer to God? What experiences have you had in Relief Society that have helped you feel or share God's love?

Questions from *God Is Hope*

1. How often do you feel foggy or overwhelmed to the point you do not feel the Spirit in your life? Do you ever wonder if God hears your cries during times of depression and anxiety? Write or share about your questioning.

2. If you wonder if God is listening, can you share how you feel when your cries seem to go unnoticed?

3. Have you ever told God you want to lay your burden at His feet and walked away in full confidence that He heard you? What changed about your feelings that day? How long did it last? When will you try again?

4. What encouragement do you need to believe that God hears your deepest cries?

5. Do you have a difficult event in your life that changed you? Did it bring you closer to God or push you away from Him? What do you think about the idea that God seeks not to hurt His daughters? Does this resonate with you, or will it require some thought and experiment to know if it is true in your life? Have you ever asked God to show His love to you?

6. Do you have an experience or image that you cling to while in times of distress? Can you draw your image?

7. When is the last time you bore your personal witness or conviction of God to yourself? Can you say it out loud? Go ahead:
   a. Do you believe your words?
   b. How did that feel?
   c. If it felt weak and ineffective, how can you care for your witness in the way you care for others in your life?
   d. If it felt good and right, can you explain your feelings?
   e. Is there something in your conviction that you'll never forget?

Notes

Notes

Notes

Notes

Notes

Notes

Notes

Notes

Notes

Notes

Notes

Notes

Endnotes

1. As Elder Erastus Snow of the Quorum of the Twelve said, "If I believe anything that God has ever said about himself . . . I must believe that deity consists of man and woman. . . . There can be no God except he is composed of the man and woman united, and there is not in all the eternities that exist, or ever will be a God in any other way. We may never hope to attain unto the eternal power and the Godhead upon any other principle . . . this Godhead composing two parts, male and female." (Erastus Snow, in *Journal of Discourses*, 19:272–73, March 3, 1878.

2. I appreciated David L. Paulsen and Martin Pulido's comments about how to reconcile the idea of Mother in Heaven with our understanding of the Godhead. They wrote, "It is no simple feat to understand how these two social relationships—the Trinity and the eternal family—can best be understood together. For one, given traditional Mormon premises, a Heavenly Mother interacts with the Trinity in a certain and irresolvable sense. As there can be no spirit children without her, presumably there would be no Son without her and perhaps no Holy Ghost—no Heavenly Mother, perhaps no Trinity. It should be no surprise, then, that most Mormon leaders could not understand how Father or Mother could be divine alone. For either to be fully God, each must have a partner with whom to share the power of endless lives." ("A Mother There: Historical Teachings and Sacred Silence," *BYU Studies*, Vol. 50 No. 1: 70–126, 2011, byustudies.byu.edu/article/a-mother-there-a-survey-of-historical-teachings-about-mother-in-heaven/

3. Interestingly a search for art featuring Heavenly Father very rarely shows him by Himself. He is almost always accompanied by either Jesus Christ or Heavenly Mother.

4. Here is the original text of the post as it was shared on April 11, 2020:

    > Have you ever noticed how in the scriptures men are always going up into the mountains to commune with God? Yet in the scriptures we hardly ever hear of women going to the mountains, and we know why—right? Because the women were too busy keeping life going; they couldn't abandon babies, meals, homes, fires, gardens, and a thousand responsibilities to make the climb into the mountains!

135

I was complaining about this to my friend Jen Mabray, telling her that even as a modern woman I feel like I'm never "free" enough from my responsibilities, never in a quiet enough, or holy enough spot to have the type of communion I want with God. Her response floored me, "That is why God comes to women. Men have to climb the mountain to meet God, but God comes to women wherever they are."

I have been pondering on her words for weeks and have searched my scriptures to see that what she said is true. God does indeed come to women where they are, when they are doing their ordinary, everyday work. He meets them at the wells where they draw water for their families, in their homes, in their kitchens, in their gardens. He comes to them as they sit beside sickbeds, as they give birth, care for the elderly, and perform necessary mourning and burial rites.

Even the women at the empty tomb, who were the first to witness Christ's resurrection, were only there because they were doing the womanly chore of properly preparing Christ's body for burial. In this seemingly mundane and ordinary task these women found themselves face to face with divinity. So if— like me—you ever start to bemoan the fact that you don't have as much time to spend in the mountains with God as you would like. Remember, God comes to women. He knows where we are and the burdens we carry. He sees us, and if we open our eyes and our hearts we will see Him, even in the most ordinary places and in the most ordinary things.

Happy Easter!

He lives.

5. churchofjesuschrist.org/study/liahona/2020/05/45nelson?lang=eng

6. Pearl S. Buck, *The Exil*, Pocket Books Inc., 1963.

7. During biblical times a man could also be "niddah" if he had a "running issue out of his flesh" (Leviticus 15:2-15). He could also become "niddah" if his "seed of copulation go out from him" (Leviticus 15:16–17), which required him to wash himself and any clothes that might have the "seed of copulation" on them. He would then be considered unclean, or in a state of "niddah," until the next day.

8. *Strongs Exhaustive Conordance*, Strongs Number G1411, blueletterbible.org/lang/Lexicon/Lexicon.cfm?strongs=G1411&t=KJV

9. Patricia T. Holland, *A Quiet Heart* (Salt Lake City: Bookcraft, 2000), 9.

10. *Saints: The Standard of Truth*, Vol. 1, (Salt Lake City: The Church of Jesus Christ of Latter-day Saints), 70–71.

11. Pirkei Avot 1:5, Sefaria: Mishnah Sotah 3:5.

12. See Matthew 27:55–56, Mark 15:40, Mark 16:1, Luke 8:1–3.

13. James E. Talmage, *Jesus the Christ*, (3rd edition, 1916), 475.

14. Jeffrey R. Holland. "Are We Not All Beggars?" [Video] Semi-Annual general conference, October, 2014.

15. Alfred Edersheim, *The Life and Times of Jesus the Messiah* (Hendrickson Publishers: 1883, reprinted 2018), 573–74.

16. Ibid., 573.

17. Rabbinic Sages debated over who was required to commemorate Biblically mandated feasts. It is understood that women in Jesus' time participated in the ritual feasts. For more information, see *Mishnah, Taanith* 4:8, and *Mishnah, Moed: Haggiah.* 1:1.

18. Evelyn T. Marshall, "Mary and Martha–Faithful Sisters, Devoted Disciples," *Ensign*, January 1987.

19. Marinella Perroni, *Gospels: Narrative and History* (Georgia: SBL Press, 2015), 365–68.

20. Isaiah (Isaiah 6:1); Moses (Exodus 3: 4–22; 33: 11); Jacob (Genesis 32:30); Abraham (Genesis 18:1)

21. Bereshith Rabbah, 45:4, attributed to Rashi, sefaria.org/Genesis.16.4?lang=bi&with=Rashi&lang2=en

22. This word can refer to mortal messengers or heavenly beings, but in those cases they are always referred to "an angel of God." For example, see Numbers 20:16, Exodus 33:2, and Exodus 23:20.

23. See "Theophany" from *Encyclopedia Brittanica Online,* britannica.com/topic/theophany

24. The KJV translates the name El-Roi as the "Thou God seest me" (Genesis 16:13). In Hebrew the word "El" means "god" and the word "Roi" means "he sees me."

25. Heinrich Friedrich Wilhelm Gesenius, *Gesenius' Hebrew-Chaldee Lexicon*, blueletterbible.org/lang/lexicon/lexicon.cfm?t=kjv&strongs=h6711

26. michaelkelley.co/2017/10/why-does-the-god-who-knows-all-still-ask-questions/

27. *Strong's Exhaustive Concordance*, Strong's number H6383, blueletterbible.org/lang/Lexicon/Lexicon.cfm?strongs=H6383&t=KJV

28. Both the word used in Judges 13:18 and Isaiah 9:6 for "wonderful" come from the same Hebrew root. In Isaiah the form of the word is a noun אלפ, while in Judges the form of the word is ‘אלפ, which is an adjective.

29. In Doctrine and Covenants 88:47 God told Joseph Smith something similar, that any person who had seen the sun, the moon, and the stars "hath seen God moving in his majesty and power," but that seeing is not always comprehending. "I say unto you, he hath seen him," D&C 88 continues, "nevertheless, he who came unto his own was not comprehended."

30. Henry B. Eyring, "O Remember, Remember," October 2007 general coference, churchofjesuschrist.org/study/general-conference/2007/10/o-remember-remember?lang=eng

31. Mount Gerizim, near Jacob's well, is considered a holy mountain to Samaritans who believed Noah came forth from the ark on the mount, Isaac was set on the altar for sacrifice, and Joseph of Egypt was buried. For further information, see Alan David Crown, Reinhard Pummer, Abraham Tal, eds., *A Companion to Samaritan Studies* (Tubingen, Germany: Mohr Siebeck, 1993).

32. The Hebrew night began at 6:00 p.m. and ended at 6:00 a.m. The night was divided into three or four watches depending on Jewish or Roman calculation.

33. Aggadic Midrash Sefaria, "Legends of the Jews," 4:3–5; see also jwa.org/encyclopedia/article/hannah-midrash-and-aggadah.

34. Living water is often associated with salvation, eternal life, and temple ritual (see Jeremiah 2:13; Isaiah 8:6; 1 Nephi 11:25).

35. James E. Talmage, *Jesus the Christ* (American Fork, UT: Covenant Communications, 2006), 165.

36. Judith R. Baskin, J"Rabbinic Reflections on the Barren Wife," *The Harvard Theological Review*, vol. 82, no. 1, 1989, 101–114, 103.

37. Ibid., 101–114, 103–104.

38. Josephus taught "a woman was inferior to her husband in all things." This helps us to understand the inferiority and marginalization of women in Jesus' timeline. Although we believe Jesus fought against the marginality of women, we must assume that her status compared to her husband's might have been very low. For more information, see Jospehus, *Against Apion,* II. 25.

39. Using an alternate translation of the Bible from the KJV can sometimes give clarity to various words in scripture. Languages are a living entity and are always in constant change and flux. The intention of observing

various approved Biblical translations is not to change the interpretation of the verse or the doctrine and principle contained therein. Because some English words have a different meaning today than when they were used in the Hebrew and Greek translation projects centuries ago, more recent Biblical translations take into account the ever-changing flux of words in a language.

40. Spencer W. Kimball, "Privileges and Responsibilities of Sisters" October 1978 general conference, churchofjesuschrist.org/study/general-conference/1978/10/privileges-and-responsibilities-of-sisters?lang=eng.

41. Josephus, *Antiquities of the Jews*, I.18.I.

42. Erika Edwards Decaster, Personal Correspondence, February 2020.

43. Pearl S. Buck, *The Exile* (Pocket Books Inc., 1963), 91.

44. The ten stories are the son of the widow of Zarephath (1 Kings 17:17–29), the son of the Shunammite woman (2 Kings 4:18–7), an Israelite man (2 Kings 4:18–7), the son of the widow of Nain (Luke 7:11–17), the daughter of Jarius (Luke 8:49–56), Lazarus (John 11:1–44), Jesus Christ (Matthew 28, Mark 16, Luke 24, John 20), Saints in Jerusalem (Matthew 27:50–54), Tabitha (Acts 9:36–42), and Eutychus (Acts 20:7–12). In the Book of Mormon we get an eleventh story, that of Timothy, who was raised from the dead by his brother Nephi (3 Nephi 7).

45. Jeffery R. Holland, October 2015 general conference, churchofjesuschrist.org/study/general-conference/2015/10/behold-thy-mother?lang=eng

46. Ibid.

47. Spencer W. Kimball, "Privileges and Responsibilities of Sisters" October 1978 general conference, churchofjesuschrist.org/study/general-conference/1978/10/privileges-and-responsibilities-of-sisters?lang=eng

48. Marion G. Romney, *Man—A Child of God, Ensign*, July 1973, churchofjesuschrist.org/study/ensign/1973/07/man-a-child-of-god?lang=eng

49. "Power of the Pack: Women Who Support Women are More Successful," *Forbes Magazine*, Mar. 6, 2019, forbes.com/sites/shelleyzalis/2019/03/06/power-of-the-pack-women-who-support-women-are-more-successful/?sh=69dde2f91771

50. Russell M. Nelson, "Woman–of Infinite Worth," Oct. 1989 general conference, churchofjesuschrist.org/study/general-conference/1989/10/woman-of-infinite-worth?lang=eng

51. Russell M. Nelson, "A Plea to My Sister," *Ensign* or *Liahona*, Nov. 2015, 95–96; emphasis added.

52. Ibid, 96.

53. Russell M. Nelson, "Sisters' Participation in the Gathering of Israel," *Ensign*, Nov. 2018, churchofjesuschrist.org/study/general-conference/2018/10/sisters-participation-in-the-gathering-of-israel?lang=eng.

54. Bruce R. McConkie, *A New Witness for the Articles of Faith* (Salt Lake City, Deseret Book, 1985), 271–72.

55. The idea of God being three individuals and yet still one is a difficult concept to grasp and one that I think our mortal brains can't quite comprehend. It is interesting that some of the most basic and foundational concepts in this world are the hardest for our minds to grasp. In languages it is often the most foundational verbs that are the most irregular and complex. For example, in English the verbs used to convey the idea of existence, such as am, are, is, being, been, was, and were, do not follow the same pattern or rules as other verbs. This is true for many other languages too. The more foundational the words are to the language, the more they stray from the normal patterns of the language. I wonder if that is also true for spiritual things—that the more foundational the concept is to our eternal existence, like the nature of God, the more complex and harder it is to understand. This doesn't mean that it is impossible to understand; it just means that it might not follow the same rules and patterns that we are accustomed to.

56. Jeffery R. Holland, *"The Only True God and Jesus Christ Whom He Hath Sent,"* October 2007 general conference. See https://www.churchofjesuschrist.org/study/general-conference/2007/10/the-only-true-god-and-jesus-christ-whom-he-hath-sent?lang=eng. Accessed Mar. 9, 2021.

57. It is significant to note that the prayer for the bread (found In Moroni 4:3) specifies that we will "always" have His Spirit to be with us, while the prayer for the water (found in Moroni 5:2) omits the "always" and simply says that we will have His Spirit to be with us.

58. churchofjesuschrist.org/study/ensign/1975/12/how-to-re.ceive-spiritual-gifts?lang=eng.

59. Russell M. Nelson, "Sisters' Participation in the Gathering of Israel", *Ensign*, November 2018, churchofjesuschrist.org/study/general-conference/2018/10/sisters-participation-in-the-gathering-of-israel?lang=eng.

60. churchofjesuschrist.org/study/general-conference/1978/10/privileges-and-responsibilities-of-sisters?lang=eng.

61. Lucy Mack Smith, History, 1845. *Joseph Smith Papers* (pp. 224–225), josephsmithpapers.org/paper-summary/lucy-mack-smith-history-1845/232.

Most readers will probably be familiar with Lucy Mack's Smith biography of Joseph Smith entitled *History of the Prophet Joseph Smith by His Mother Lucy Mack Smith*. This book, published by The Church of Jesus Christ of Latter-day Saints in 1902, was not Lucy's original work. It was abridged by George Albert Smith. Her original manuscript was written, and a few copies published, in 1845. This original manuscript has more stories and details than the abridged version published in 1902. The story I have shared here is not found in the 1902 version, only in the later 1845 edition, which can be read online at the *Joseph Smith Papers* website.

62. You can follow Sarah Frei on Instagram @ strong.like.sarah. She is very open about her story and willing to share how she has reached to God in all her struggles. Sarah is seventeen, bright, beautiful, and works hard every day to navigate her new normal. In the strength of Christ, we pray for and with Sarah that she will continue to be sustained and sanctified through the lifelong challenges that are now on her shoulders.

63. Selections from John 20:15, Romans 12:12, John 16:7, and John 14:18–19.

64. Those who heard Jesus cry out thought he called for Elijah, since Eli is not a traditional name to use for God in Hebrew. Sadly, after He cried out, some-one filled a sponge of sour or bitter wine, which is the token petition for Elijah to return, and offered it to Jesus to drink. Afterward, he and others in their mocking attitude waited to see if Elijah would come to save Him. Shortly thereafter, the text in Matthew tells us Jesus cried with a loud voice and then passed away.

65. See Young Women Theme, churchofjesuschrist.org/study/manual/young-women-theme/young-women-theme?lang=eng

66. Joseph Fielding Smith and George D. Pyper, "Does the Journey Seem Long?" Hymn Book, Church of Jesus Christ of Latter-day Saints, 1973, *Hymns of The Church of Jesus Christ of Latter-day Saints* (Salt Lake City: The Church of Jesus Christ of Latter-day Saints, 1985), 127.

67. Joseph Fielding Smith and George D. Pyper, "Does the Journey Seem Long?" Hymn Book, Church of Jesus Christ of Latter-day Saints, 1973, *Hymns of The Church of Jesus Christ of Latter-day Saints* (Salt Lake City: The Church of Jesus Christ of Latter-day Saints, 1985), 127.

68. United States Holocaust Memorial Museum, "Ravenbrück," Holocaust Encyclopedia, encyclopedia.ushmm.org/content/en/article/ravensbrueck. Accessed Jan. 15, 2021.

69. Sara Tuvel Bernstein, *The Seamstress* (The Penguin Group, 1997).

70. Ibid., 228.

71. This phrase was said by Seren in various ways in her memoir. She used it to convince herself she could make it, and to convince Lily, Esther, and

Ellen to stay alive. Lily closed her eyes and died in Seren's arms, while Seren begged her not to die, not to give up. Despite Lily's death, Seren still held onto the hope that she, Esther, and Ellen would "refuse to die."

72. Sara Tuvel Bernstein, *The Seamstress*, 259–261.

73. Ibid., 256.

74. Ibid., 273.

75. Ibid.

76. See Martin Luther King, Jr., *In My Own Words*.

77. See Young Women Theme, churchofjesuschrist.org/study/manual/young-women-theme/young-women-theme?lang=eng.

78. Laurel Thatcher-Ulrich, *Well Behaved Women Seldom Make History* (Knopf Doubleday Publishing Group, 2008), XXXII.

About the Author

Heather Farrell

*H*eather Farrell's love of the scriptures began young when, at the age of eleven, she hid a flashlight under her pillow so she could read the Old Testament late at night. Her love for the women in the scriptures began when her oldest son was born around Christmastime and she felt a kinship with Mary, the mother of Jesus.

As Heather began to research Mary, she realized there were hundreds of women in the scriptures, but very little had been written about them at the time. Excited by all the women she discovered, she began sharing what she learned on her website, Women in the Scriptures (womeninthescriptures.com).

Heather is a testament to the truth that becoming a scholar of the gospel is not beyond anyone's reach. It just takes an inquisitive mind and the companionship of the Holy Ghost.

Heather's other books include *Walking with the Women of the New Testament*, *Walking with the Women of the Old Testament*, *Walking with the Women of the Book of Mormon*, and *The Gift of Giving Life: Rediscovering the Divine Nature of Pregnancy and Birth*.

Heather lives in Pocatello, Idaho, with her husband and six children.

About the Author

Jen Mabray

Jen is a recent MA graduate of Jewish Studies and Hebrew from Washington University in St. Louis and has accepted a position as a PhD student at Saint Louis University where she will work on the intertextuality of women in the Hebrew Bible and Midrash (Jewish literature).

In her personal life, Jen is happily married to her very best friend, Todd. Together they have four amazing children and are so pleased with who they are becoming.

Additionally, Jen is the owner of a commercial and editorial photography company, is in her eighth year as a seminary teacher for The Church of Jesus Christ of Latter-day Saints, and enjoys playing the piano and listening to books on Audible.